RADICAL DISCIPLE

Radical Disciple

The Influence and Significance of John J. Vincent

Festschrift and Testament

EDITED BY

Ian K. Duffield and
Robert P. Hoch-Yidokodiltona

WIPF & STOCK · Eugene, Oregon

RADICAL DISCIPLE
The Influence and Significance of John J. Vincent: Festschrift and Testament

Copyright © 2025 Wipf and Stock Publishers. All rights reserved. Except for brief quotations in critical publications or reviews, no part of this book may be reproduced in any manner without prior written permission from the publisher. Write: Permissions, Wipf and Stock Publishers, 199 W. 8th Ave., Suite 3, Eugene, OR 97401.

Wipf & Stock
An Imprint of Wipf and Stock Publishers
199 W. 8th Ave., Suite 3
Eugene, OR 97401

www.wipfandstock.com

PAPERBACK ISBN: 978-1-6667-1210-0
HARDCOVER ISBN: 978-1-6667-1211-7
EBOOK ISBN: 978-1-6667-1212-4

Scripture quotations are from the Revised Standard Version of the Bible, copyright © 1952 by the Division of Christian Education of the National Council of the Churches of Christ in the United States of America. Used by permission. All rights reserved.

"But go, tell his disciples and Peter that Jesus is going ahead of you to Galilee; there you will see him, as he told you."

—Mark 16:7

Contents

Preface | *Robert Hoch-Yidokodiltona* | xi
Acknowledgments | *Ian K. Duffield and Robert Hoch-Yidokodiltona* | xv
Introduction | *Ian K. Duffield* | 1

PART I
The Primacy of Situation

Orientation to the Primacy of Situation | *Ian K. Duffield* | 9
1. "Welcome to Sheffield"—Blaming It on John Vincent | *Noel Irwin* | 12
2. Your Place, Your Church, Your Group, and Situation Analysis | *Robin Pagan* | 19
3. Keeping Faith in the City: How UTU Played a Part | *Alan Billings* | 26

PART II
The Primacy of the City

Orientation to the Primacy of the City | *Ian K. Duffield* | 39
4. Urban Mission and Ministry | *Terry Drummond* | 42
5. Renewing the Church Through Gospel Projects | *Geoffrey B. Curtiss* | 48
6. Christ in the City in El Salvador | *Tony Crisp* | 56

PART III
The Primacy of Discipleship

Orientation to the Primacy of Discipleship | *Ian K. Duffield* | 67
7. Journey with John: Disciple, Scholar, and Friend | *Nirmal Fernando* | 69
8. Discipleship, Context, and Lived Religion | *James Curry* | 73
9. John Vincent's Alternative Church | *Christine Dutton* | 76

Contents

PART IV
The Primacy of Mark's Gospel

Orientation to the Primacy of Mark's Gospel | *Ian K. Duffield* | 85

10. Meeting John Vincent: Context, Witness, and Radical Humility | *Kevin Ellis* | 88
11. John Vincent, Mark's Gospel, and the Fusion of Horizons | *David McLoughlin* | 94
12. Vincent's Radical Markan Project | *James Bullock* | 98

PART V
The Primacy of Practice

Orientation to the Primacy of Practice | *Ian K. Duffield* | 115

13. Living Mark's Gospel in New England: Urban Ministry Projects | *Don Rudalevige* | 119
14. John's Contribution to Ministerial Training | *Christine Jones* | 125
15. Emmaus Road in Birmingham: Galilee in Sheffield | *Ruth Weston* | 132

PART VI
The Primacy of Radical Christianity

Orientation to the Primacy of Radical Christianity | *Ian K. Duffield* | 141

16. A Journey of Theological Self-Discovery | *Joe Aldred* | 145
17. The Testimony of Jesus: Anticipate the Ethics of the New Age | *Chris Rowland* | 153
18. The Integrity of the UTU Method | *Laurie Green* | 163

PART VII
Short Personal Tributes, Testaments, and Testimonials

19. Eye-Openers | *Margaret Mackley* | 175
20. Crossing the City | *Frances Morgan* | 178
21. The Tale of Two Drew-Ids | *John David Dillon* | 180
22. St. Francis House | *Anne Scheibner* | 181
23. Embodying the Radical Spirit | *Richard Firth* | 183
24. Completing the Circle | *Andrea Misler* | 185
25. The Best Colleague | *Ian Lucraft* | 187

Contents

APPENDICES

I. Biography of John James Vincent | Robert P. Hoch-Yidokodiltona | 193
II. Select Bibliography of John James Vincent | 198

Preface

IN THE GOSPELS, JESUS compares the kingdom of God with the mustard seed, the tiniest of all seeds, which grows to produce a great tree with a generous canopy—its branches provide not only for itself but for the diversities of the world. It speaks not only of the kingdom but of kingdoms. It shows the capacity to not only be a thing in itself, but to give to many others, including a diverse range of creatures and ways of being, a base community that, in turn, sustains a form of life unique to each. This feels like an apt description of John Vincent's influence in the theological world and for the world God so loves.

Some theologians may exercise a larger influence than John, but few could claim to have set into motion the diversity of vocations represented in this volume. Of course, you find the usual suspects, including theologians and pastors—and their contributions speak of John's work in ways that readers will find inspiring as well as familiar. But you will also hear the testimony of a police commissioner, a birth activist, a head teacher, a clinical psychologist, and others. These diverse vocations offer accounts of how John's breadth and generosity—which he would assign to the radical Jesus, the tiniest of seeds—gave shape to their development in what he calls the "practical divinity" of Jesus of Nazareth.

I am also in this diverse canopy of witnesses, though as "one lately born." I moved from a pastorate in inner-city Baltimore, Maryland, to the UK, near my wife's family, in December 2020. Among other things, my roots include being a mixed culture indigenous person from North America and a member of the squatter community known as Hippie Cove in Cordova, Alaska. I've always found it ironic that an indigenous person would ever need to describe themselves as a "squatter" in North America, but that's what I was and maybe still am wherever I live.

Preface

Obviously, my interests in theology followed a different path from John's, but in some ways I feel a kindred spirit with him. My work, *By the Rivers of Babylon: Blueprint for a Church in Exile*, would, I like to think, have been of interest to John, especially the way in which community, through radical fidelity to God's commitment to the poor, arises as a way of challenging the worst aspects of exile. All that to say, before moving to the UK permanently, I did not know John Vincent, or the UTU, or even Sheffield. For me, John's legacy, the Urban Theology Union, felt like a piece of driftwood, something that you see and it feels curious, maybe familiar with its knots and bends, but not quite fitting into any settled category. You take it with you, a kind of hanger-on, but it comes to feel more like companion than artifact. It finds a place in your garden, and it tells its story quietly through its presence. Maybe that's how I would describe my experience of UTU, something collected from the sea and its foam, something chance swept in and that chance might have swept out.

On a whim, while looking at UTU's website, I sent off my CV, not expecting to hear back, but in less than a week, Erica Dunmow, chair of the board, emailed back and asked if I'd like to have a talk about our respective visions for theological education. Things moved quickly from there.

In June of 2021, I met John at his home in Sheffield for the first time. He was eager to talk, even as he closed in on his ninetieth year. I learned that Karl Barth, a name I know well, had served on his doctoral committee. They could not be more different theologically—John tells me that Barth disagreed with his thesis but respected his argument. Although a world apart theologically, these two shared a generosity of spirit that flows through their respective legacies. But it would be wrong to say that John's legacy was in any way that of a traditional theologian, as he himself admits: "All liberation theology is contextual, so my theology is a liberation theology based on my context. . . . So I seek to be a disciple in the inner city and theologise on the basis of it."[1] He is also unashamed of this gospel, boasting that UTU, at one point in its history, was the only theological college with outside toilets.[2] John brings some mischief, a vigorous struggle for justice, and a determination to test theological education against the grit of street, neighborhood, and social policy—that prophetic call challenges the traditional norms of academic theology. The context for discipleship, not the

---

1. Vincent, *Christ in the City*, 30.
2. Vincent, *Christ in the City*, 25.

classroom as such, would be the proving ground for the theological project he imagined.

Soon, I would be teaching a certificate course with John, and getting a firsthand experience of the founder of UTU. Knowing John in the classroom, listening to him think through Mark's Gospel, and his occasional surprise at what he finds in the Jesus of Mark, has been a rare privilege. However, I would say that I know John more deeply through the people who have known and been shaped by him. I hope that even these readers, familiar as they are with John, will discover some new insights into what motivated him, and those who have not known him, except through indirect knowledge, will be inspired to continue the legacy of his vision for contextual theology.

By now, you can probably guess that this book is not a traditional Festschrift in which the contributors map out the scholarly influence of their thinker—and argue here and there with the direction of that legacy. This is not that book. Instead, this book bears the stamp of testimony or even testament of those who knew John as a fellow disciple. They bear witness to something he fully expected they would grow from and through and, indeed, shape in their own vocational development. This volume bears witness to the person alongside the theological orientation, the spirit with the words, the tradition of contextual theology, and the people who came to shape it as their own—and their testimony to the person who welcomed them on a journey into a vocation as diverse and varied as the promises of God.

This prayer, from the *Book of Common Worship: Daily Prayer*, comes to mind as I think of John's life and the legacy of his work recorded in this book:

> Eternal God,
> you call us to ventures
> of which we cannot see the ending,
> by paths yet untrodden,
> through perils unknown.
> Give us faith to go out with courage,
> not knowing where we go,
> but only that your hand is leading us
> and your love supporting us;
> through Jesus Christ our Lord. Amen.[3]

---

3. Theology and Worship Ministry, *Book of Common Worship*, 39.

I suppose that this prayer, or one like it, has been on the lips of most if not all the people who have been influenced by John. And I also suspect there might have been a quiet smile of satisfaction when, under John's influence, they "gave it a go" for the world God so loves.

Rev. Dr. Robert P. Hoch-Yidokodiltona (United Reformed Church) is mixed culture, Athabascan and White. He is registered as a direct lineal descendant with the Eyak and Chugach Natives of Alaska. He serves as UTU's director of Theological Studies (2001 to present). He lives near Pendle Hill in Lancashire.

Bibliography

Hoch, Robert P. *By the Rivers of Babylon: Blueprint for a Church in Exile*. Minneapolis: Fortress, 2013.
Theology and Worship Ministry Unit, The. *Book of Common Worship: Daily Prayer*. Louisville: Westminster John Knox, 1993.
Vincent, John J. *Christ in the City*. Sheffield: Urban Theology Unity, 2013.

Acknowledgments

This book would not have been possible without the generous support of Urban Theology Union's loyal donors and dedicated volunteers, including its board of trustees, as well as those members who support its day-to-day operations: Erica Dunmow, chair of the board; Andrew Crowley, treasurer; Joe Forde, human resources; and Ruth Weston, communications. Their work alongside that of the board of trustees continues to remind us of the strength and resilience of John Vincent's vision for church and academy. We would be remiss if we neglected to express our debt to Jill Wagg, UTU's office manager. Although her name does not appear in the list of contributors, be assured that her contributions helped to bring this project to the finishing line as, without fail, she helped us with correspondence, scans, and other materials we requested along the way. Jill does much that we do see and much, much more that we don't—Jill's warmth, hospitality, and timely communications keep the work of UTU humming along efficiently and cheerfully.

We would also like to acknowledge Victoria Hall Methodist Church for housing UTU's library and PhD seminars. Maurice Stafford's encyclopedic knowledge of John's publications provided invaluable help in the bibliography. Additional thanks go to those who supplied photographs, including Christopher Vincent, Neil Manthorpe, and Margaret Mackley. Their photos give us a glimpse of the person who continues to inspire and provoke radical discipleship even to this day. Christopher and James Vincent contributed personal reminisces that are included in the biography for John in the appendices. Not least, our contributors, students, friends, and companions of John: they consistently give the reader both a personal and theological account of John's place in their callings and ministries. Through their contributions, we meet scholar, prophet, friend, and mentor.

Acknowledgments

Any acknowledgment is imperfect, and this one is no different. It could take up many pages trying to be complete, and yet it would remain incomplete. It would be like trying to count the stars or carefully numbering the grains of sand in a desert . . . or trying to include all the stories that could be told . . . there are not enough books in the world to hold them all.

Introduction

IN 1997 WE PRODUCED a volume entitled *Urban Christ*, which was a series of responses to John Vincent from friends and colleagues at UTU and beyond.[1] This was a small attempt to honour John on his retirement as director of the Urban Theology Unit. Of course, retirement is not an apt word to describe John. As director emeritus he has, until recently, continued to tutor, lecture, and supervise since then, as well as continuing to write articles and books, not least to pioneer some new practice-based avenues of biblical exploration.

In the introduction to that volume, we explained that this was a way of participating in the European academic tradition of the Festschrift albeit in a distinctive, UTU-type way. The same is true for these contributions, which constitute something of an alternative Festschrift. These are not essays primarily written around John's concerns or an opportunity to present a case that the writer wishes to put forward or to enter into debate with John, but records of John's influence and impact, of his significance for us. In that sense they are more of a testament.

So, we have brought together semi-autobiographical essays that highlight the influence of John and UTU for their own lives and ministries and that, at the same time, record elements of UTU's history (see, for example, Laurie Green's evocation of the early days of UTU, and Christine Jones on ministerial training at UTU) and stories of John as a colleague (see, for example, the offerings by Nirmal Fernando and Ian Lucraft), or as a supervisor (see, for example, Andrea Misler and James Curry), plus John's impact through his thought and writings (see, for example, Noel Irwin and Joe Aldred), which indicate something of his significance to the church, to the academy, to the kingdom, that is, to encourage gospel-shaped mission and discipleship in our day. Hence, in these offerings we are given insights

1. Duffield, *Urban Christ*.

into John and his style through cameos, or a historical reminiscence, or a testimony to his influence, or a tribute to his impact. As John says: "Testament is just what this person or couple or group have chosen to set down. They cannot deny it, it just happened some way, like this."[2]

Of course, this is only a partial record, because a book can be only so long, but we hope that these contributions capture something of the elusive and mercurial, the pioneering and maverick, the entrepreneurial and radical disciple John Vincent. Indeed, John's own writings often inadequately communicate his passionate and enthusiastic and engrossing speech, what Joe Aldred calls his "mature excitableness," which, like a good preacher, stimulates and challenges—opening and closing doors, turning over tables, stimulating vocation, provoking responses, encouraging radical discipleship—an exciting, at times almost breathless experience, but always full of depth, insight, and alternative perspectives, whether it's on Mark's Gospel or politics, the church or existential social realities, biblical interpretation or the urban. On the difficulties of characterizing this remarkable minister, theologian, biblical scholar, and disciple of Christ, see my attempt that follows this introduction.

The volume is roughly structured around some distinctive and key Vincentian themes that attempt to encapsulate at least something of the person, and his life, and his mission. As these themes or trajectories tend to be dynamically interlinked, there is an inevitable artificiality to the way the contributions are collated, and we beg the forgiveness of contributors if they think we've got it wrong. Nonetheless, we thought it helpful to try to delineate the material, if only to break up the text and to establish some order even though, as we know well, at UTU, crucible reactions and dynamic processes and human creativity cannot be pinned down, as John himself cannot be pinned down.

Of Pillars and Primacies: Vincentian Foundations

Behind the phenomenon that is John Vincent we may discern certain foundations, although these are too dynamic and interactive in practice to be able to bear the weight of this word. So, although John in his June 24 presidential address identified five pillars that needed to be taken seriously by the Methodist Church, I shall call them "primacies" to name commitments and approaches and assumptions that can help us to delineate the

---

2. Vincent and Vincent, *Inner City Testament*, 9.

INTRODUCTION

phenomenon that is John J. Vincent. At UTU we are particularly interested in investigating phenomena in our doctoral program, i.e., realities with which we have to do, which stand before us in all their resistant uniqueness and idiosyncrasy.[3]

In this Festschrift, "John's primacies" are placed in a rough sequence and demarcate the different parts of the volume with an orientation by myself, at each point, that will indicate John's language and refer to his writings to substantiate their significance for understanding him and relate them to each other and to my own experience as well as that of others. Some may wish to read all these introductions before moving towards the particular contributions, to gain a sense of the whole. Otherwise, each introduction assists an orientation to what is to follow in each part and includes my own personal reflections.

The structure is based around some key primacies that may be said to characterize John's approach, and which need to be understood to understand John. These foundations are outlined below. Each part of the volume will include a personal introduction or orientation to the particular primacy by Ian, indicating what it points to and where it can be found in John's speech and writings. This is followed by contributions, which may be more or less related to the primacy in question—at least, in part of what is said. But because these primacies are somewhat interlocking or at least interrelated, each primacy will be found to have a place in other parts of the book as well.

The parts are as follows:

Part 1: "The Primacy of Situation"—or "situation analysis," which highlights the importance of location and place as the context from which one understands the world and acts upon it.

Part 2: "The Primacy of the City"—highlighting the new discipline or activity that John invented, "urban theology," which he increasingly calls "urban theologizing," which reflects upon analysis of the inner city where vocation is located and enacted.

Part 3: "The Primacy of Discipleship"—highlighting the key theme from John's doctorate to Ashram Community that characterizes his own vocation and his own self-understanding and to which he calls people.

---

3. For example, take John's two final PhD students that he supervised at UTU for Birmingham University: Andrea Misler's thesis investigated the unique Othona Community situated in Essex and James Curry researched the realities of lived religion of Episcopalians in Upper Deeside.

Part 4: "The Primacy of Mark's Gospel"—highlighting John's own personal inexhaustible canon, which undergirds his understanding of every other primacy and the source of his understanding of both gospel and gospel projects.

Part 5: "The Primacy of Practice"—highlighting the significance of practice over or before theory or theology, and hence John's encouragement of projects or, more correctly, gospel projects; and the subsequent development of the new academic discipline of "gospel practice criticism" or "practice interpretation" that John has pioneered and encouraged, whereby practice is preeminently understood as evoked by and rooted in Scripture and at the same time also becomes an interpretative tool of it.

Part 6: "The Primacy of Radical Christianity"—highlighting John's view of himself as a "radical" of the "radical Jesus" and his approach to Christianity as "radical Christianity," and hence of the need for radical practice and radical discipleship in the church as evidenced by liberation theology.

Finally, we have updated the bibliography and biography of John contained in *Urban Christ*, to put them on record, as it were. Although this does not contain everything, it is a reasonably comprehensive presentation, which on its own indicates something of John's significance. Certainly, if one wants to explore further, resources are handily gathered here. Though, as we said earlier, John's writings never quite convey the man and the impact he can have on you when you hear him speak and are enthused by his approach and challenged or provoked by his rhetoric. Above all, John is always inviting people to walk alongside, to embrace their vocation where they are, to become disciples of the urban Christ, to take the journey downward, to engage with Mark's Gospel as a liberating text that for those with eyes to see and ears to hear can direct mission in our day, to respond with gospel projects, to enact the kingdom in the here and now, and to discover that our radical practice feeds back into our reading of Scripture, ever anew, so that new outworkings of the gospel emerge.

What history or theology will make of John J. Vincent in the future is unknown, but we offer this record, this collegial testament, of what we make of him in 2024, in the belief that he has a place in the Third Testament that is continuously being produced of writings worthy to be accepted by Christians since the closing of the New Testament, along with John Wesley and many others.

Introduction

How to Describe John Vincent—That's the Question

John Vincent is like a great oak tree: he casts a giant shadow, and it's virtually impossible for those who have studied under him or worked with him to escape his abiding presence—and how can one talk about UTU or urban theology or Ashram Community without talking about him?

John Vincent is like a spiritual guru who founds an ashram and advocates discipleship and is someone to whom one looks for wisdom and insight, but who does not have his own disciples because he has only colleagues and collaborators and encourages them to be disciples like the first disciples, but above all disciples in the urban; and is sometimes so provocative that he puts people off.

John Vincent is like a theological Yokozuna (from the world of Sumo wrestling), who has so many skills and moves one is constantly in awe of his ability and agility in the face of changing circumstances; like other sporting greats, it's as if he sees things more quickly or notices spaces that others miss and can exploit maneuvers that others wouldn't dream of exploiting.

John Vincent is like a prima donna (from the world of opera), as Canon Eric James said to me when consulting him about studying under John; but as Eric said, John is a particularly good prima donna, and he encouraged me to come to UTU back in 1980 when I started considering urban ministry to listen to this distinctive voice with such a range that it can take your breath away.

John Vincent is like a great maestro who not only composes music that's distinctively their own and conducts the orchestra, but can play every instrument, including some of his own design; yet who encourages others to learn or design a new instrument themselves, to write their own music or to compose a riff on his own compositions, and characteristically treats people as colleagues, compatriots, and comrades in a common endeavor, and models his way of doing theology by luring people into making theology with him in collectives and collaborations, intentional communities and alternative congregations.

John Vincent is like a throwback to the prophets of old, who were often provocative or objectionable and who inevitably challenged their listeners to go to where the people were by going there himself.

John Vincent is a Methodist in tension with Methodism, its enfant terrible, who was yet a loyal son who came to Sheffield where he was stationed even though it did not accord with his hopes and plans; John the Methodist who was not bound by Methodism and yet resourced by it sought to remind Methodists of their inheritance and its outworking in a secular world, themes that appear throughout his writings. When John was made president of the Methodist Conference I was privileged to be there and to witness the holy moment when the Wesley Bible is handed from the past president to the new one. At this sacred point it was as if Wesley was with us once again as John's countenance revealed the arc of Wesley.

John Vincent the radical theologian who points toward "a new Reformation" and the ongoing significance of protest within the uncertainties of our time; the dangerous theologian who eschewed a full academic career, which beckoned after his doctorate in Basel with the internationally known Oscar Cullmann, and instead opened a backyard seminary on the opposite side of the city (in many senses) to the university, and pioneered groundbreaking approaches to Scripture encouraging everyone to engage in endogenous theology, in a new mutation of theology, to be their own theologian and writer like himself.

John Vincent the persistent student of Mark's Gospel as a radical text—the ultimate radical canon within a canon (going far beyond Marcion)—who endlessly revisits the text year by year and plumbs its depths where he finds it yields fruit, with barely a thought for any other Scripture; a narrowness and tightness of vision that continues to reveal vistas unseen by others. Mark is the key text by which he seeks to discipline others in the journey into discipleship and through which he engages with the mysteries of the radical Jesus.

Not surprisingly, therefore, this volume does not seek to describe John Vincent, but to witness to his legacy as the Radical Disciple.

Rev. Dr. Ian K. Duffield: Anglican priest, DMin (1983), core staff (1985–2019), director of UTU (2009–13), director of research at UTU (1997–present)

Bibliography

Duffield, Ian K., ed. *Urban Christ: Responses to John Vincent*. Sheffield: UTU, 1997.
Vincent, John J., and Grace Vincent. *Inner City Testament: Changing the World from the Bottom*. Sheffield: Ashram, 2017.

PART I
The Primacy of Situation

Orientation to the Primacy of Situation

Ian K. Duffield

John often says: "Who you are is where you are."[1] I had discovered the truth of this before I heard John say it. I was ministering in one of the most privileged towns in the country (the land of Eric Morecambe and Terry Wogan) when I heard the call to the urban. Although I'd not heard of what John calls "urban discipleship," I nevertheless felt the vocational call toward it. And it was thinking I ought to get some training before I ministered in the urban that I discovered UTU and its urban ministry course. Then, when I first met John in 1980 and he interviewed me in the narrow basement corridor of the UTU library at 210, he recruited me for the doctor of ministry (DMin) program at the same time. And on his encouragement, I left the leafy streets of Hertfordshire commuter land and moved with my young family to Sheffield and to the impoverished streets of the Manor Estate, where the primary school that our lads attended was unfairly labeled the worst in England.

That the "situation" or "context" has primacy for John is evident in the first of his "city" trilogy.[2] And it lay behind his clarion call, which was adopted by the Methodist Church in the 1980s: Mission Alongside the Poor.[3]

Situation analysis has been a "pillar" of the UTU approach and manifests that UTU, among other things, is about doing theology contextually, which is why UTU easily became a constituent college of Luther King House in offering degrees in contextual theology in the 2000s. This focus is

---

1. Vincent, *Jesus Thing*, 37.

2. Vincent, *Into the City*.

3. Note the significance of "alongside"—see Paul Keeble's MPhil thesis, supervised by John, published as *Mission With*.

Introduction to Part I

particularly apparent in UTU's earlier development of the master of ministry and theology in the 1990s with which I was involved for many a year, not least in helping students do situation analysis in their specific contexts.

My understanding and recollection of events is thus: John, who had "invented" the process very early on, instigated its use with New York Theological Seminary (NYTS) for the UK version of the DMin that began at UTU in the late 1970s (see Laurie Green's contribution)—an innovation: the first DMin to be offered in Britain; and perhaps the only DMin of its kind, as the degrees that now go under that title in the UK are more professional doctorate than action-research. When UTU pioneered the master of ministry and theology in the UK, situation analysis was naturally incorporated in the degree that was validated by Sheffield University. It began as a master's (alongside a bachelor's for those training for the ministry; see Christine Jones's contribution), on the wise and friendly advice of Professor John Rogerson of the Biblical Studies Department, with a later upgrading to a DMin in ministry and theology that mirrored more the British academic tradition, which became the first DMin of any kind validated by a British university. And it was for the master of ministry and theology that Christine Dodd (the Roman Catholic adult education advisor in the Diocese of Hallam, and UTU/NYTS DMin graduate) did her revision of the document (which Robin Pagan discusses) as one of the supervisors of the program.

So, situation analysis was embedded in the process that led to an action-research project that was vital to the DMin approach and John's enthusiasm for participants to engage in a contextually relevant gospel project, which was also key to the master's of ministry and theology, where students developed a project proposal that was then put into effect. Eventually, Sheffield University agreed that this could be upgraded to a DMin in ministry and theology, whereby a thesis was developed in the light of the preceding work. The evolution of this degree as a distinct academic innovation, pioneered by UTU with Sheffield University, demonstrates the centrality of situation analysis to UTU's approach, whether it's at diploma level or at various degree levels. It is a primary indicator of the significance of situation analysis as a necessary prelude to gospel action/program/project for John and for UTU, and as (generated by John) an important long-term influence on all those who've studied at UTU and learned this contextual procedure/process that forces one to engage with particular realities can be applied in every place (not only the urban).[4] In the 1980s, to run alongside situation analysis we also encouraged folk to work on social and structural analysis.[5]

Bibliography

Duffield, Ian K., ed. *Contextual Analysis*. Sheffield: UTU, 2018.
———. "Urban Theology: Location, Vocation, and Action." In *Faithfulness in the City*, edited by John J. Vincent, 266–79. New York: Monad, 2003.
Keeble, Paul. *Mission With: Something Out of the Ordinary*. Watford, UK: Instant Apostle, 2017.
Vincent, John. *The Jesus Thing: An Experiment in Discipleship*. Nashville: Abingdon, 1973.
———. *Into the City*. London: Epworth, 1982.

---

4. I have written more generally on the significance of location (i.e., situation/context) for the doing of theology in Duffield, "Urban Theology."

5. See Duffield, *Contextual Analysis*, 13–19.

1

"Welcome to Sheffield"— Blaming It on John Vincent

Noel Irwin

Growing up in Belfast during the Troubles, I developed a passion for social justice—causing rows at home and hassle in the Methodist Church that I was brought up in. Indeed, the Christian faith I was hearing about in church and was trying to live out in following Jesus seemed to have no relevance to the violence and the injustice occurring daily on the streets of Northern Ireland, or in other places in the world I was learning about, like apartheid South Africa. I heard a lot about sin, but it was a very clearly limited, personal sense of sin—don't drink, don't smoke, etc. Jamie Malan writes about South Africa, and these are words rightly applied to the situation in Northern Ireland:

> It is astounding how many good Christians in our land are ready to acknowledge before God that they are sinners, but who become angry if anyone suggests that their confession of guilt should include those parts of our political structure which by promoting our privilege at the expense of others, undercut the moral integrity of our people. Or will they try to assert that such things do not exist?[1]

Looking back, there were a couple of things that kept me in the church. First, I had a wonderful religious education (RE) teacher in school, Charlie Kenny, who somehow managed to get into the O and A level curriculum:

---

1. Hannon, *Whose Side Is God On?*, 37.

Christian socialism; liberation theology; Bonhoeffer; Bultmann and Harnack. The other thing was I came across a little book by John Vincent called *O.K., Let's Be Methodists*, which connected me to a tradition in my church that said to me, "Yes, you actually belong here," and how a concern for social justice affirmed a legitimate focus for a Methodist. I must admit the first sermon I ever preached was based much more on this book than on the Bible. After I met John in person for the first time in 1999, I said to him I blamed him for me hanging on in there as part of the Methodist Church!

First Impressions: My Trade Unionist Dad

While I was aware of John through his writing, my Trade Unionist father was impressed with this Methodist minister who stood up to Margaret Thatcher in his year as president of the Methodist Church in Britain in 1989. In fact, it is the only time I can ever remember him cheering a clergyman when John appeared on TV criticizing the Christian veneer Thatcher was trying to provide for her policies. Rod Garner rightly says about John's work that it provides us with "a living reminder that theological thought is inescapably political. It must always be concerned with who is doing what to whom, for good or ill, in our own rapidly changing times."[2]

In his books John spoke about this place in Sheffield called the Urban Theology Unit (UTU). I remember writing off to UTU (ah, the days before the internet!) for a leaflet; the courses looked amazing, and I thought it would be fantastic to study with John. I saw that one of the things UTU did was train Methodist ministers, and as I was in the process of candidating for the Irish Methodist ministry, I thought (naively) it might be possible for me to do my studies in Sheffield with John at UTU. No such luck, of course, and it was to be another ten years or so before I wrote to John Vincent about doing "some research" and he invited me to come over for the summer schools on liberation and urban theology. I think his exact words were "Come to Sheffield." Here began an almost twenty-five-year association with UTU as a PhD student, member, graduate, tutor, and finally director.

---

2. Garner, *Facing the City*, 18.

John and Grace

It was on that trip I first received wonderful hospitality in John's house, down the street from UTU, and met his wife Grace for the first time. Grace picked up on my Belfast accent very quickly, and we chatted about her dad, who was a Methodist minister in Ireland (I had known of him), her time at school in Methodist College Belfast, Queen's University Belfast, and my research interest on the Troubles. John then became my main PhD supervisor. When I began to travel over to Sheffield from Belfast for supervisions every three months, I would stay in UTU, but Grace would often feed me in their house.

Spending time with John, I quickly realized a few things: one was the amazing breadth and depth of his intellect; then there was how the political and justice commitments that burst onto the national stage in 1989 were forged first of all in Sheffield; also their (John and Grace were as one in this) absolute commitment to the gospel journey downward (John's expression) into their context.

John has a first-class mind, which, I imagine, could have gained him lectureships and chairs in top universities throughout the world. However, one of the most Methodist things I saw in John was his commitment to what Wesley spoke of as "practical divinity," which had no place for idle speculative thought. Theology was always to be turned to practical service for both John Wesley and John Vincent. For me, in contrast, I love philosophy; I find it fascinating to think about God until my head hurts; and I also love the book of Revelation. These three areas John just refused, point-blank, to talk about—I am absolutely sure the expression "arty farty" was frequently used by him. Yet, I have a prized possession of a very hefty tome of process theological thought, pre-owned by John, passed to me as "more your sort of thing," with copious insightful notes throughout the whole volume. John absolutely could do the speculative stuff, but he was so much more about theology and indeed biblical study (OK, Mark!) being a critical reflection on praxis.

David Price suggests that the prominent role the Labour Party played in Sheffield during the 1980s was influenced by John Vincent.[3] Many folk connected with UTU were involved in the struggles of the miners in the strike of 1984–85. Brian Jenner wrote a book in 1986, published by UTU, providing, as its subtitle indicated, *Christian Reflections on the Miners'*

---

3. Price, *Sheffield Troublemakers*, 154.

Struggle.[4] As visitors, students, lecturers, and friends started to come from all over the world, UTU was reminded that the struggle for justice and the rule of God was not just contextual but also inter-contextual, as Andrew Davey emphasizes: "Local pastoral praxis becomes simultaneously global political praxis."[5]

What a praxis it was. I decided to apply for a job in Sheffield, and even before I had the interview John wrote in the flyleaf of his new book, *Hope from the City*, in June 2000, "Welcome to Sheffield." He had a lot more confidence in me than I had in myself! But, now living in Sheffield, I saw John and Grace's incredible commitment and appetite for work in Ashram, Sheffield Inner City Ecumenical Mission, the two New Roots shops, and, of course, constant helping out around UTU with whatever needed done, whether it was practical or academic, plus there was a complete immersion from them in a deprived community.

In 2015–16 we moved from Sheffield to Manchester; I commuted over for a couple of days per week when I was in my final year as UTU director. John and Grace kindly invited me to stay with them whenever I needed. John and I would talk after Grace had gone to bed, and he would make me porridge in the morning. Now Grace is gone, I shall always really treasure those times and the stories shared.

My Debt to John

I owe John so much. I had a stroke in 2004. John was the first clergyperson to visit me in hospital—I could not speak—he prayed with me and cried. I remember the boot being on the other foot when John had a heart problem and was put in a high dependency unit. I happened to be in the hospital, and I went in to see him. When I asked a nurse where he was, she pointed him out and asked if it would be possible for me to stop him correcting papers when he was hooked up to all the machines. I said I would try, but I doubted any of us could stop him!

I would not have gotten my PhD without him as my supervisor—especially his deep pastoral care and concern for me after the stroke, when I was unsure if I would ever speak properly or preach again, never mind write a blessed doctorate. John showed incredible patience, helping for a year to get my writing back up to a suitable standard. It is thanks to John

4. Jenner, *Coal Strike*.
5. Davey, *Urban Christianity*, 39.

I managed to get the blessed doctorate without requiring any corrections at all.

In 2003, when I became the superintendent of Victoria Hall, the Methodist mission in Sheffield city center, John moved from a supervisor who gave me the encouragement, space, and nurture to develop my own theological and biblical thought, to someone who did exactly the same thing for my ministry without pushing his agenda on me at all. He was always there with guidance when needed and pastoral care when I did not think I needed it but actually did. John baptized our son in that church, and he was deeply loved and valued by all the congregation, for all he did in supporting my ministry and the mission of Victoria Hall.

There's Only One John Vincent

A note about UTU at the end of Brian Jenner's book talks of how UTU built itself up "from the bottom" to try to serve this need (the liberation and empowerment of the common people and their servants, the Christians). It is based on a sharing-caring community, almost wholly unpaid, of men and women who live in two or three pleasant but undeniably inner-city streets of northeast Sheffield.[6] Here we see the strength of the urban theology developed by John at and through UTU, which was built up "from the bottom" with a DNA for social justice—this is something I longed for from being a teenager in East Belfast and was grateful to find it in John and in UTU. As someone who now works training church-related community workers for the United Reformed Church, there is still a great need for John's approach to theology today as churches have withdrawn from city centers, inner cities, and housing estates. Talking of the Methodist Church and speaking trenchantly, John said:

> We have deserted the poor. The last sixty years of Methodism in Britain indicate consistent policies. We deserted the working-class areas and took our chapels, along with our money, into the suburbs . . . we sold off our downtown, inner-city, and street corner chapels, and used the proceeds for ministry for ourselves. We silenced our prophets and wrote statements of political correctness rather than prophecy. . . . We gave bits of money to Mission Alongside the Poor, but mainly never put our bodies there. . . . We

---

6. Jenner, *Coal Strike*, 95.

stopped calling people to mission, sold our central halls, and used the profits to fund ministries of "presence," without people.[7]

Sadly, I do not see that much has changed since John wrote these words.

If we look at John's life and work, we see a unique contribution in terms of scholarship and gospel practice to British Methodism and Christianity—there really is only one John Vincent. Sadly, with the structures of the contemporary church obsessed by structures, management, business, and homogeneity, I am convinced we will never be allowed to see the likes of John Vincent again.

I am so thankful for knowing John, just finding someone who in their writing and then in life had a commitment to social justice that matched and developed my own concerns made a huge difference to me. I think the words attributed to William Temple, "When I pray, coincidences happen," could well be applied to the way John came into and stayed in my life. As Ken Leech says: it is difficult to exaggerate the contribution that Vincent and the UTU have made to the understanding of urban theology, and there are thousands of people throughout the world who have been helped by this project in Sheffield.[8]

I am proudly one of them.

Rev. Dr. Noel Irwin: PhD graduate, tutor in public theology and church-related community work, Northern College, Luther King Centre for Theology and Ministry, and former director of UTU

Bibliography

Davey, Andrew. *Urban Christianity and Global Order: Theological Resources for an Urban Future.* London: SPCK, 2001.
Garner, Rod. *Facing the City: Urban Mission in the 21st Century.* London: Epworth, 2004.
Hannon, Peter. *Whose Side Is God On? By an Enquirer in Northern Ireland.* Self-published, 1995.
Jenner, Brian. *The Coal Strike: Christian Reflections on the Miners' Struggle.* Sheffield: UTU, 1986.
Leech, Kenneth. *Through Our Long Exile.* London: Dartman, Longman, & Todd, 2001.
Price, David. *Sheffield Troublemakers: Rebels and Radicals in Sheffield History.* West Sussex: Phillimore, 2008.

7. Vincent, "Basics of Radical Methodism," 33.

8. Leech, *Through Our Long Exile*, 133.

Vincent, John. "Basics of Radical Methodism." In *Methodist and Radical: Rejuvenating a Tradition*, edited by Joerg Rieger and John Vincent, 31–49. Sherborne, UK: Kingswood, 2004.
Vincent, John J. *O.K., Let's Be Methodists*. London: Epworth, 1984.

2

Your Place, Your Church, Your Group, and Situation Analysis

Robin Pagan

I FIRST BECAME AWARE of the Urban Theology Unit (as it then was) when I picked up a copy of *Stirrings*, edited by John J. Vincent, back in 1980. This was when I was attending at a rather tepid national conference that had left me somewhat underwhelmed. Reading the essays enthused me, and I took up the invitation at the end of the book to contact UTU for further information. Within a few days I received a letter from John Vincent inviting me to join a group who would be considering the possibility of becoming involved in the doctor of ministry (DMin) program that he was arranging in conjunction with New York Theological Seminary (NYTS). As I had already considered the possibility of postgraduate study but had found what was on offer unsuitable for my pastoral ministry, e.g., esoteric research themes and attendance requirements hardly suited to the pastoral ministry in which I was involved, John's offer was very welcome, and I subsequently found myself a member of the 1981 intake of doctoral students at UTU. The rest, as they say, is history, or at least my history with UTU, which is still going on forty years later!

A Special Ethos

I give these autobiographical details in the best UTU tradition of providing some context to what follows, but more significantly, I believe, as an indication of some of the special qualities of the UTU ethos that contrasts so sharply with that of the more established places offering postgraduate study, and in doing so reflects not just on UTU as an institution but also on the personality of John himself. So, the self-publicity of UTU is at the heart of its endeavors, and not only was the book made available, but the invitation at the end continued the connection. And then, of course, the invitation to consider the doctoral program, not knowing anything about me, is so typical of John's proactivity. All of this contrasting with the ways of the established schools of learning, where all that was to be heard was the sound of doors closing.

This openness to all to explore their calling through the rigors of study remains an essential part of UTU. Early on in our meetings as the doctor of ministry cohort of 1981, I was surprised to find out that this openness of John and the institution required a reciprocal openness from ourselves; as students as we were asked to share something of ourselves and background in one of the early sessions. This may not seem very radical, but it made me realize that I couldn't remember having participated in such an exercise before in any other educational environment. I remember feeling personally valued and already part of a group, sharing in the adventure of learning and practice that lay ahead. At that time, we occasionally indulged in completing personality tests and the like, but I think the important thing about this approach was not so much a desire for inward self-knowledge but as a basis for a developing group dynamic with its cooperative ethic, which has been essential to John's style.

Situational Analysis: A Rehearsal

In this contribution to the celebration of John J. Vincent and UTU, I will attempt to rehearse some of John's insights and qualities alongside the place of UTU by considering two early, and formational, documents/worksheets entitled "Situation Analysis" and "You, Your Group, and Your Place." In the second of these papers by Edward S. Kessler, known more informally as Ed and an early supporter of John and the UTU project, we are invited to just such an exercise. "Now, tell yourself the most important thing about you," he asks. No small task, but again it is important to remember that this is not an exercise in inwardness but to be understood as one aspect of ministerial dynamics, the others being "Your Group" and "Your Place" in all their variety and limitations. With the aid of a three-winged diagram we are shown how these three components are to be understood in a dynamic relationship, which, when thrown into the crucible of ministerial analysis, can reveal where significant action can be taken. So,

> the dynamics of your "programme," the "thing" that it is about, will lie in the "overlaps" of the three ministerial components already mentioned and where the itch occurs between them, that the nature of your "programme" becomes apparent. So, if the "itch" is between "You and Your Place" you will be most profitably involved in a "community/development programme," or if between "You and Your Group" then in a "ministry/congregational programme," and if between "Your Group and Your Place" in a "life style/prophetic programme."[1]

In summary, Ed requires us to ask the question of just how radical our program is and comments:

> Some might suggest that this is all radical or irrelevant nonsense, that we must get back to traditional jobs of the church. . . . Or, some might suggest that the gospel has little to do with the whole operation. . . . We are not in conflict with the traditional model of church . . . [but we] shall suggest that the gospel has a great deal to do with "Community Development" or "Ministry/Congregational" programmes, in their purpose, method and personnel.[2]

My involvement in Ed's urban ministry course was to run in parallel with my first year on the DMin at UTU with John as my supervisor and Dick Snyder as a visiting supervisor from NYTS. We managed to get a group together for the urban ministry course and had our first meeting in Newcastle upon Tyne, which was central to where we severally ministered. I had known the church some years before as a somewhat prim and proper Gothicized building and was surprised to find the elegant interior plastered with posters declaiming the rights and wrongs of all things Central American. The session seemed to go well, and I was looking forward to the next session, only to find out that our host was not able to stay in the group and so the group folded. I suspect that he was already clear about his "program" and realized that he didn't have time for the course. Again, I add this little bit of autobiography to illustrate something of the insecurity that is part of being a small establishment with limited budget and few, largely voluntary

---

1. Kessler, "You, Your Group," 1.
2. Kessler, "You, Your Group," 3.

helpers. These aspects of UTU's existence have been characteristic of its being and seemingly necessary for its ongoing independence.

Ed summarizes his paper thus:

> YOU we are "stuck with," so to speak (and glad to have). Going through the urban ministry course should result in some deeper understanding of yourself, though there is no intention on our part of playing at psychiatry or the like . . . YOUR GROUP may not exist yet and will to some extent be determined by you, your place, and the defined program for ministry . . . YOUR PLACE you are "stuck with," so to speak, whether it be a congregation or a neighbourhood or an institution, and it is here that we will concentrate the work of our SITUATION ANALYSIS.[3]

This leads us to the consideration of our second UTU paper/worksheet of that name formulated by John.

Of all the UTU worksheets, documents, etc—and there are quite a number—the situation analysis document is the one that has been central to the UTU pedagogical approach.[4] It is interesting to note that the copy in my study is subheaded "By John J. Vincent (1973) with Revisions by Christine Dodd (1991)," which not only reminds us of the document's longevity but also of John's openness and encouragement of others to make their contribution to the program. The latest adaptation of this document can be found in *Contextual Analysis*, edited by Ian K. Duffield.[5] Following on from the previous paper/worksheet, the situation analysis paper/worksheet is divided into three parts: your place; your community; and your church, plus an important final section entitled "When You've Done It All."

"Your Place" is a joy for those of us who enjoy maps and mapping (although with GPS we may be a dying breed) and assumes that a large-scale street map of the area is made available. In order to do this honestly it is important to suspend belief in your current knowledge as infallible. I am reminded of being taken on a tour of some of the massive docks in London's East End by a local minister in the early eighties only for him to be shocked by the lack of any ships or activity. He hadn't been there for some years, and things had moved on or, should I say, moved downstream. The moral being that situation analysis is an ongoing requirement of ministry

---

3. Kessler, "You, Your Group," 2.
4. Vincent, "Situation Analysis."
5. John J. Vincent, "Situation Analysis," revised by Christine Dodd and Ian K. Duffield, in Duffield, *Contextual Analysis*, 3–10.

and requires constant updating. Under "Your Place" the worksheet requires the patient mapping of roads (major and minor, etc.), buildings, housing (private, council, etc.), residents (elderly, young married, single, etc.), ethnic groups, demolition areas, and the catchall "Any Other Features." Obviously, every situation is different, and this list is indicative rather than final and should encourage the practitioner to add complementary information as the situation demands. If this exercise is done with proper humility, it is surprising what new insights can arise and how long held tropes can be challenged.

Under "Your Community" things tend to move on from simple mapping to areas of evaluation, but even or, should I say, especially here, subjective evaluations need to be based on objective criteria. So, for example, the first section "People" is again a matter of gathering facts: Who are they? What sort of jobs do they have? But as we move on, the headings assume more soft, evaluative information under "Relationships," "Perceptions," "Recent Experiences," "Lifestyle."[6] This section closes with some interesting if challenging methods that might be tried to get this information, such as "hanging around pubs, talking outside schools, welfare clinics." If you have survived this experience and have not been arrested in these less innocent days, there are more formal methods such as surveys, questionnaires, etc., which help to give more objective information.

The "Your Church" section follows a similar pattern, beginning with those boring facts that you think you know already, until that is, you begin to begin to write them down. So, when asked what churches there are in your area, it's very easy just to list your own along with those of the mainstream traditions, but given the growing diversity of our society, this exercise requires a deliberate effort to seek out those congregations lying beneath our conventional radar. It's surprising what gems are waiting to be discovered. The wider question regarding "ecclesiastical structures and boundaries" is also important if any interchurch project is to run smoothly. Then come a list of things regarding your local church: "staff ordained or lay," "lay leadership," "church membership" (and such things as its age profile), and "fringe members" and their contribution. Further questions ask about patterns of worship, church activities, facilities of the premises, and financial situation and projections. Again, these things become clearer

---

6. For anyone considering this likely to be a boring task, I invite them to read *People of Providence*, by Tony Parker, that dedicated recorder of vox populi. I can honestly say I have never looked at a high-rise apartment block in the same way ever again!

when a deliberate attempt is made to list them in the here and now and not as it might have been ten or fifteen years ago. Deeper questions arise under the section headed "Portrait of the Church Community," which kicks off with what is sometimes a touchy area: "What is the relationship of the leadership to the congregation?" Further questions about "cliques or affinity groups" and "decision-making, theoretically and practically" indicate that this is no facile exercise but one that demands a high degree of honesty and integrity on all those participating. There are some fifteen items listed in this section on the life of the local church, and, while these cover the main areas of church life, there is no reason why any church getting involved in the process of responding to them should not add their own. I leave with number 11: "Religious ethos: What is the overall feeling? What is the impact on a stranger?" The stranger and the wider world concern the subject of the final area of preparatory work of analysis required before moving on to planning any such program: "What," we are asked, "in your world, place and community is the church supporting? (Good or bad) What is it trying to change? What could it support or change?"

So, we come to the end of the analytical work prescribed by John's "Situation Analysis" worksheet, and it would appear that some groups that have been involved in the demanding exercises outlined here end up with so much information that they feel overwhelmed by it, as articulated in the sigh of desperation; what others call "analysis paralysis." But this happens only if the information gleaned is seen as an end in itself and not as a means to a greater end. The final section of the worksheet, "When You've Done It All," which is fundamental to the way John thinks, leads into the next and crucial phase of program development or project creation with the exercise "Ten for Sorrow, Ten for Joy" and ends with proper humility, suggesting, "Then perhaps you'll begin to say. 'We could do something about . . . couldn't we?'"

Testimonial: Why We Play

I hope this somewhat abbreviated outline of the sort of work that was basic to UTU and John's pedagogy has rung a few bells with those who have been involved and whetted the appetites of those who may want to find out more. In testimonial mode I would like to affirm how important this manner of thinking about ministry and shaping it to the context has been to me from my first exposure to it in the DMin program through my various ministries in rural, suburban, and city center situations. I have also had the privilege of working with UTU's master of ministry and theology degree (validated by the University of Sheffield), which was modeled on the DMin, which, of course, began with situation analysis, and I've also worked with doctoral students, in the several different guises the doctoral program has had to adopt, but always seeking to keep this search for the contextual realities central to research and to any project arising.

In conclusion I return to Ed—John's sidekick back in the day—and his document, where under the heading, "Why Play at All" he lists the following six reasons:

1. You will (in the best sense of the word) "enjoy" your ministry more.
2. You will do some good things.
3. You will get others to do some good things.
4. You will find a new dimension to ministry.
5. You will help others to find new dimensions to their ministry.
6. You will get on to something new and big.

I think I'll go along with that.

Rev. Dr. Robin Pagan: URC minister, DMin (1983), core staff (1985–2019), PhD supervisor

Bibliography

Duffield, Ian K., ed. *Contextual Analysis*. Sheffield: UTU, 2018.
Kessler, Edward S. "You, Your Group, and Your Place." Urban Theology Worksheet. 1974.
Parker, Tony. *The People of Providence: A Housing Estate and Some of Its Inhabitants*. 2nd ed. London: Eland, 1983.
Vincent, John J., ed. *Stirrings: Essays Christian and Radical*. City Soundings. London: Epworth, 1976.
Vincent, John J. "Situation Analysis." Urban Theology Worksheet. 1973. Revised by Christine Dodd, 1991.

3

Keeping Faith in the City: How UTU Played a Part

Alan Billings

John Vincent has probably never known how important the methods he taught at the Urban Theology Unit (UTU) were for my own life and ministry—until now. But without them I would not have been able to make as useful a contribution to the 1985 Church of England report *Faith in the City*.[1]

In 1981 there were serious riots in a number of English cities—places like Brixton in London and Toxteth in Liverpool. Cabinet ministers in Margaret Thatcher's government seemed nonplussed and paralyzed. The archbishop of Canterbury, Robert Runcie, was deeply disturbed and resolved to set up an inquiry of his own to help both church and nation understand what had happened. What had caused the riots? What were the causes of the causes? What could be done to ensure nothing like this happened again? He asked eighteen men and women to form the Archbishop's Commission on Urban Priority Areas (ACUPA) and to make recommendations to both church and nation. What might not have been appreciated was the part that the thinking of John Vincent had on some of the commission's work and legacy—which I will come back to.

The methodology of the commission is worth noting. Each commission member brought to the task some area of expertise arising from our day-to-day working lives—in housing, community development, health,

---

1. Commission on Urban Priority Areas, *Faith in the City*.

social care, education, local government, business, order, and law. The chair was the former head of the Manpower Services Commission (MSC), Sir Richard O'Brien. The MSC headquarters were, of course, based in Sheffield, and the iconic pyramid-shaped building stands at the end of the moor. Our secretary was seconded from the Department of the Environment. I was asked to be on the commission as an inner-city parish priest and also because I was deputy leader of Sheffield City Council and knew something about local government. The bishop who proposed me also knew that I drew a lot of my inspiration from UTU and John Vincent, whose talks and lectures I described then, and still think of now, as "provocations"—they forced you to think.

Provocations and Faith in the City

I count myself as very fortunate in that, by chance, when I came to take up my first job after curacy, I found myself in the same city as UTU and could often drop into 210 Abbeyfield Road. For me in my urban priority area (UPA) parish—Broomhall—John's provocations were a lifeline. They sent me back to the Scriptures and made me think in a way I had hardly done since leaving theological college. Like a former principal of Kelham Hall (Society of the Sacred Mission)—a place that was also important to me at one time—I started my working day with my mind moving between biblical passages and *Guardian* editorials—though I am not sure it was the *Manchester Guardian* that Fr. Herbert Kelly read.

The commission consisted of men and women, old and young, Black, White, from different parts of the country, and many different backgrounds. In effect we created our own think tank at a time when such organizations were not as prolific as they are now. We asked local authorities to tell us where their most deprived communities were and then spent two years between 1983 and 1985 going round some of the poorest parts of the country, looking, listening, learning. We felt that this was vital. We needed to experience directly what we called "the human reality behind the official statistics." This was a costly decision in terms of both time and finance—but the right one. It meant that when we came to publish the report it carried a good deal of weight: we represented a broad range of Christian perspectives, we knew what we were talking about, and we reported from the front line. We had what today would be called lived experience.

Sometimes we had full plenary sessions with all eighteen of us pooling our knowledge and receiving presentations and papers from academics and other experts, including government and local government officials from the various places we visited. At other times we traveled in twos to meet as many people and organizations as we could. I often accompanied the bishop of Liverpool, David Sheppard, and our task was focused in large part on what sustained the Urban Priority Area (UPA) churches, their laity and clergy: What was their underlying theology? The bishop was an Evangelical, and I was from the Catholic wing of the Church of England, and this enabled us to speak to those from each of those constituencies with a certain ease and fluency.

I have vivid memories even now of particular encounters. On one occasion I went with the bishop to meet an evangelical vicar in inner London. Tower blocks surrounded his vicarage. There was a great deal of concrete, very little green space, and no trees. His congregation was small. When we called, there had just been a gathering of Evangelicals from all over the country in a nearby church to talk about conversions and growth. It had made him depressed because he did not have a success story to tell. The bishop tried to cheer him up. He might not have big numbers, but if he thought in percentage terms he was probably just as successful as some of the bigger churches. Tears formed in the young vicar's eyes as he did the maths. His congregation had shrunk by 20 percent since he had come. I think that was probably the moment I realized that a church that sees mission exclusively in terms of growth in a secularizing age is going to leave many of its members and supporters in the same depressed place as this inner-city vicar. Where was the theology that would enable him and his congregation to go forward with some confidence whatever their numbers? That, of course, remains an issue for the contemporary church.

I also recall going with the bishop to part of his own diocese, Kirkby in Liverpool. This was a vast estate and many of those living there had been rehoused from the center of Liverpool. The police, I recall, went around in twos. I stayed with an Anglo-Catholic family who told me that when they lived in Liverpool and the Orange marches were held, they had their windows put in because they were not proper Protestants, and when the Irish nationalists marched, they had their windows put in because they were not proper Catholics! I went with them and the bishop to a community meeting in a youth center that had been opened by Harold Wilson. The hall was packed—as halls were everywhere we went. Toward the end, one man stood up and in a broad scouse accent thanked us for coming but pointed out that Liverpool had received every government initiative since the war—and he listed them all—and there was still unemployment, poverty, and lack of opportunity. If he were alive today, he might say the same.

One of the great strengths of the Church of England at that time was that it had a presence—buildings, clergy, and congregations—in every part of the country. Its clergy and laity were deeply involved in the general life of their communities and not just in church organizations. So, between 1983 and 1985, we had access to people in each urban center and their firsthand experience. By the end of two years we were able to give some voice to those who are not normally heard and to put into words what others vaguely understood but couldn't quite put their finger on. One decision we took was to include some direct quotations from the people we met—something that is now routinely done in reports but at that time was fairly novel.

Like a Bombshell

Our final report, *Faith in the City: A Call for Action by Church and Nation*, was critical of government policy failures and fell—to adapt Karl Adams— "like a bombshell in the [politicians'] playground." The government tried to discredit both the report and the commission members. In a television interview, Norman Tebbit, a cabinet minister, described me as the "Marxist" deputy leader of Sheffield City Council. My fellow councilors thought this was very funny because I was regarded as on the right of Labour politics— though my stock probably rose as a result. Of course, the contemporary Church of England is in process of throwing all these strengths away as it turns its back on the parish system—despite denials—and stumbles toward a different model of the church that will reduce its presence in today's equivalent of the UPAs.[2]

Discovery, Truth, and Outcomes

What did the commission find? I think we made one important discovery and underlined one important truth.

---

2. A transplanted or grafted congregation is not the same as an indigenous UPA congregation—and that probably points up the difference between then and now and what has been lost since *Faith in the City*.

The discovery was this: prior to *Faith in the City*, poverty was thought to be an inner-city problem. Government's attention focused on those Victorian and Edwardian terraced houses that ringed the city centers. There was indeed poverty in the inner city. But in concentrating all our attention there we had not noticed what was happening behind our backs on the outer estates, much further from the center. The commission spoke about urban priority areas and not just inner cities. UPAs could be anywhere.

The truth we underlined was this. Left to itself, every economy distributes benefits and burdens unequally—largely a consequence of where older industries are dying and newer ones flourishing. But a society will remain cohesive only if steps are taken to share the benefits and shoulder the burdens more equally. That was and remains a primary task of government. And that is no longer an issue between the major parties. The previous Conservative Government's "levelling up" agenda signifies just that. Of course, whether it was effective is another matter.

Faith in the City had one very important outcome for the Church of England. It created the Church Urban Fund, which enabled churchgoers in more comfortable Britain to support people and projects in places that were struggling. That was the Christian gospel in action, a way of loving your neighbor when your neighbor lives at a distance. And the fund enabled many parish churches to adapt their premises or fund staff so that they were better able to serve their communities.

Theological Implications

Toward the end of our time, as we began to think about the shape of the report and what should go in it, we reflected a little on the social theology by which—mainly unconsciously—we had been guided. A chapter on theology was eventually included in the report: "Theological Priorities." But this chapter was written after the main work was completed and was not really the theology that motivated us. Indeed, it was far more hesitant than that, perhaps because the writer was a New Testament scholar rather than a theologian.

The report took the form it did because we consciously rejected at least one approach. We rejected the idea that somehow Christians should constitute communities of protest, standing over against mainstream society as a counterculture. We were not persuaded by the sort of thinking that emerged, for example, with Stanley Hauerwas—and his more radical idea of Christians as resident aliens. The Pauline text "Whilst we have time, let us do good unto all people, especially those of the household of faith" (Gal 6:10) did not imply for us an exclusive concern for the Christian community. While the more radical Christian may play a role from time to time in recalling Christians to some basic truths of the gospel, this type of Christian witness is always on the periphery of society. We were provoked more by Jeremiah and his letter to the exiles (Jer 29) that we should seek the welfare of the city—get stuck in and involved. Our concerns were with the political order of the day and the need to bring about change in the here and now, and the here and now is the plural world of Christian and non-Christian. And we were, after all, the established Church of England, committed to work with government, local and national, where we can.

We were influenced to some extent by Roman Catholic social teaching. One of our members, who was a Roman Catholic, Robina Rafferty, the assistant director of the Catholic Housing Aid Society, frequently drew upon it, especially the idea of the common good. But our principal source of inspiration was the tradition of Anglican social thinking associated with William Temple. Indeed, one of the commission's advisers was Canon Dr. John Atherton from the William Temple Foundation. Our methodology was that used by William Temple and those who collaborated with him in the interwar, wartime, and immediately postwar period. We were influenced by the idea of middle axioms and the thinking that led to Temple's little book *Christianity and Social Order*, which was so influential in the church and beyond when it appeared in 1942, selling almost 140,000 copies. I had read Temple as an undergraduate and continued to read those who maintained the tradition subsequently, especially Ronald Preston. This was the real social theology of *Faith in the City*.

We spoke in the introduction to the report of justice and compassion. On the whole, we sought to find a middle ground between general statements about social and economic justice and detailed policies. We wanted to offer both Christians and non-Christians general guidance in the face of the glaring (and the hidden) inequalities and injustices of the urban priority areas. Looking back almost forty years on, I think we were looking for something in the sphere of economics and social policy that was equivalent to the idea of just war in military ethics, though we never put it that way—a way of framing questions, a template, for any society at any moment in time to measure itself against. But we also wanted to see how that worked out for our society at that particular time. As a result, I think the report became more detailed than we originally expected and than many would have liked.

There were other factors that drove us to make more detailed recommendations. Some of us were already deeply involved in the political life of our cities and knew that change could come about only if we could persuade politicians to make particular policy choices. Making grand statements was not enough. We also knew that many of the issues we encountered were not being discussed in either our churches or in society more generally. But we had spent two years listening to the voices of people in the UPAs where our presence had raised expectations that we would come up with at least some concrete proposals and make the case to government. Many told us that they felt powerless and had no voice: we must be their voice. The report inevitably moved in the direction of detailed proposals.

Looking Back: Criticism, Questions, and Legacies

It was seen, as I have said, as an attack on the policies of the Thatcher government, though we had tried to say that we found fault with all governments. Where I do think we made a mistake was in not listening carefully enough to the voices of those Christians and others who recognized the problems of the UPAs but did not share what turned out to be the unanimous view of the commission that a large part of the answer had to be state intervention. After the report was published, we received criticism from both the religious and the political right.

A Christian academic critic was Brian Griffiths, now Lord Griffiths, who believed that wealth had first to be generated—largely through private enterprise—before it could be redistributed, and there was little acknowledgment of that in the report. Margaret Thatcher believed this as well as her exegesis of the parable of the Good Samaritan on one occasion makes clear. The Good Samaritan had first to earn the money that he used to support the man who had fallen among thieves. Griffiths went on to become director of the No. 10 Policy Unit.

But the most severe religious critique came from Immanuel Jacobovits (1921–99), the chief rabbi of the United Hebrew Congregations of the Commonwealth. He wrote a short riposte, *From Doom to Hope*, essentially arguing against state intervention and for greater resilience on the part of the unemployed. They should be more determined to find jobs wherever they were and work hard. They should follow the example of the Jews who had been displaced in Europe at the turn of the twentieth century and come to Britain with nothing. Through hard work they had achieved prosperity. He also pointed to the importance of the family as a basic building block of a secure and prosperous society.

Margaret Thatcher found this much more appealing than the message of *Faith in the City*, saying on one occasion that she wished the chief rabbi were the archbishop of Canterbury. Perhaps it was not surprising that she gave Jacobovits a seat in the House of Lords. These were voices that we had not heard on our travels. Nor was this perspective represented on the commission. If it had been, it would have been more difficult to produce a unanimous report though it might have led to some tighter arguments.

We were determined that the report should have concrete outcomes and not simply be politely received and left to gather dust on a few shelves in libraries and studies. Politically the report raised awareness of the plight of the UPAs and created such a stir nationally that no politician could ignore the issues. The prime minister, Margaret Thatcher, said on the eve of her third election victory in 1987, "We must do something about those inner cities."[3] For the church, I have already mentioned the Church Urban Fund. This was created in 1987 as a direct result of the report. It was initially hoped that £18 million might be found over a twenty-year period. But by 1996, £25 million had been raised and more than 1,180 projects supported in UPAs across the country.

A second legacy is often overlooked—the church audit. This was where my association with the Urban Theology Unit and John Vincent played a role. Commission members often spoke about the way some local churches were better at understanding their local context than others. I said at one meeting that it would be good to enable all UPA churches to undertake what at UTU we called a "situation analysis." To anyone who had been through John's courses at UTU, doing such an analysis had become second nature. Whenever I moved from one church to another, I always took the church council or the whole congregation through such an analysis.

I explained to the commission what a situation analysis involved, and we quickly agreed that this would be a good thing for churches to do. As we were to write in the report, "It would help a church to understand itself in its situation, to reflect on its purpose, and then to make plans for becoming

---

3. Johnston, "Our Cities," para. 1.

a more effective, outward-looking and participating church."[4] We called this "An Audit for the Local Church."

The audit had two parts. Part 1 helped the local church to understand its context, and part 2 enabled it to make future plans. We borrowed shamelessly from techniques that I had learned from John. We said, for example, that as well as assembling various statistics about the parish—principally around the demographics—the local church should seek to find out how people in those different demographics felt about the area. We recommended a brainstorming session on the ten things people most liked and most disliked about the place—"ten for sorrow, ten for joy." I recall John also saying that as revealing as the lists themselves was the speed with which people put their joys and sorrows forward: if they were quick to speak about their joys, that was a hopeful sign; but if they struggled, that was not. (When I traveled around with David Sheppard gathering evidence, we sometimes used "ten for sorrow, ten for joy" at community meetings.)

I think the audit was as important a gift to the churches as the Church Urban Fund. After publication I was invited to many UPA churches to speak about the findings—as were all the commission members. I found them already attempting the audit or planning to do so. The exercise opened many eyes and led to many initiatives for serving the parish better. I recall contributing something toward the last words on the audit and quoting Cardinal Newman:

> Inevitably deep questions will arise about the nature and purpose of the church and the meaning of the Christian gospel. People should be encouraged to face them, even if there is disagreement, as long as the discussion leads to action and is not an evasion of it. A sufficient common mind is needed simply for the next step. "I do not ask to see the distant scene, one step enough for me."[5]

The report had personal consequences for me. I was invited to join the staff of Ripon College, Cuddesdon, becoming vice principal and director of the Oxford Institute for Church and Society. My mission was to set up a base in Sheffield where Anglican ordinands who had theology degrees could spend time in a UPA parish learning and applying the techniques of situation analysis. I had been deputy leader of Sheffield City Council before leaving for Oxford so used my previous contacts at the council to

---

4. Commission on Urban Priority Areas, *Faith in the City*, 92.

5. Commission on Urban Priority Areas, *Faith in the City*, 372; quoting John Henry Newman, "Lead, Kindly Light," st. 1.

help secure a house in St. Swithun's Parish on the Manor Estate. It was a pattern of Anglican formation that was subsequently copied by other colleges, such as Westcott House. Here, future parish clergy learned the approach of situation analysis so that it would become second nature for them as they left for parish ministry.

The indirect influence of UTU and John Vincent on the Church of England is not often recognized. What I have tried to do in this chapter is set out some of that as it affected me and some of the things I did during my time as a parish priest. At different times, John's provocations have made me pause and think, given me inspiration and motivation, and, above all, kept me sane.

Canon Dr. Alan Billings: DMin graduate, PhD supervisor, author, former police and crime commissioner for South Yorkshire

Bibliography

Commission on Urban Priority Areas. *Faith in the City: A Call for Action by Church and Nation; The Report by the Archbishop of Canterbury's Commission on Urban Priority Areas.* London: Church House Publishing, 1985.

Jacobovits, Immanuel. *From Doom to Hope: A Jewish View on the "Faith in the City," the Report of the Archbishop of Canterbury's Commission on Urban Priority Areas.* [London?]: Office of the Chief Rabbi, 1986.

Johnston, Philip. "Our Cities Must Be Freed to Flourish Again." *Telegraph*, Mar. 18, 2013. https://www.telegraph.co.uk/news/politics/conservative/9937818/Our-cities-must-be-freed-to-flourish-again.html.

Newman, John Henry. "Lead, Kindly Light, amid the Encircling Gloom." Hymnary, 1833. https://hymnary.org/text/lead_kindly_light_amid_the_encircling_gl.

Temple, William. *Christianity and Social Order.* New York: Penguin, 1942.

PART II

The Primacy of the City

Introduction

Orientation to the Primacy of the City

Ian K. Duffield

John coined the term "urban theology" and hence the key descriptor of his backyard seminary, or alternative theological educational enterprise: The Urban Theology Unit or, as it is known today, the Urban Theology Union.

At the same time, John often talks about "starting at the bottom." This situation or context animates John, and, in that key, he speaks of "Urban Realities" in the important volume of essays he edited, *Faithfulness in the City*.[1] So, the situation or context or location that has primacy for him is the urban, hence his development of "urban theology" (or "urban theologizing").[2]

The other way John indicates the significance of the urban is by privileging the city, which is particularly evident in his city trilogy: *Into the City* (1982), *Hope from the City* (2000), *Christ in the City* (2013). But by the city, he privileges "the bottom," namely, the inner city or other similar areas of multiple deprivation. Advancing liberation theology's focus on the poor (e.g., Jon Sobrino's *The True Church and the Poor*), John regards this location as privileged, so he can talk about *Gospel from the City* (1997), the title

---

1. See Vincent, *Faithfulness in the City*, ch. 2.

2. See the third of his city trilogy, *Christ in the City*. UTU in practice has been the generator of most of its forms of urban theology, even if it's possible to link John to one specific form. In any case, as doing urban theology is more about process, it inevitably changes with different contexts, so one should expect it to take varied forms (see Duffield, "Process and Practice").

of the second volume of *British Liberation Theology*, co-edited with Chris Rowland.

Many of his writings indicate a focus on the city. For example, the joint volume he wrote with John Rogerson, *The City in Biblical Perspective* (2014), part of the series Biblical Challenges in the Contemporary World. Then there was his earlier involvement in *The Cities: A Methodist Report* (1997), what may be regarded as a Methodist version of *Faith in the City* for the 1990s, which he co-chaired.[3] And then there were occasional forays and campaigns. So back in 1980 John and Roy Crowder initiated a "Call to Home Mission," which led to a working party and the production of *Two Nations, One Gospel?* presented to the 1981 Methodist Conference on the growing divisions in society.[4] From this flowed the Mission Alongside the Poor campaign adopted by the 1983 conference, and prior to that, in the same year, *A Petition of Distress from the Cities* (1983) calling for a change of policies that might "lead to the liberation, flourishing and empowerment of all."[5] So, although John and UTU have been willing to work with non-urban folk and have found that our methods and processes can work well with people from a vast range of different circumstances and situations, it is the urban that provides the touchstone.

Although others may want to talk about the city in its entirety (e.g., Andrew Davey's writings), John focuses on the inner city, the bottom, which constitutes the prime meaning of "city" for him. For John, incarnation takes flesh where flesh is under pressure. So much so that he can talk of "becoming flesh in Grimesthorpe."[6] No doubt this is why he has devoted his life to a particular location within Sheffield, on the opposite side of the city to the universities and to the wealthy, where he still lives to this day. The inner city is for him the prime location in which to do theology, to discover vocation, to be a disciple, to enact gospel things, which leads naturally to the next primacy.

---

3. Methodist Working Group, *Cities*.
4. Inner City Committee, *Two Nations, One Gospel?*, 2.
5. Home Mission Division, *Petition of Distress*, 1.
6. This is the title of an article in the *Methodist Recorder* (Nov. 28, 1996), referring to where John and his wife Grace had set up a storefront church. Further bibliographic information unavailable.

Introduction to Part II

Bibliography

Duffield, Ian K. "The Process and Practice of Urban Theology." *Franciscan* 31 (2019), 3, 7.

Home Mission Division, Urban Mission Consultation. *A Petition of Distress from the Cities*. Sheffield: New City, UTU, 1983.

Inner City Committee of the Division of Home Mission Working Group. *Two Nations, One Gospel?* Sheffield: New City, UTU, 1981.

Methodist Working Group on the Cities, The. *The Cities: A Methodist Report*. London: Methodist Church and NCH Action for Children, 1997.

Sobrino, Jon. *The True Church and the Poor*. Translated by Matthew J. O'Connell. Maryknoll, NY: Orbis, 1984.

Vincent, John J., ed. *Faithfulness in the City*. New York: Monad, 2003.

———. *Christ in the City: The Dynamics of Christ in Urban Theological Practice*. Sheffield: UTU, 2013.

4

Urban Mission and Ministry

Terry Drummond

I FIRST MET JOHN Vincent on a spring day in 1972. At the time I was a Church Army student on a placement with the parish of Christ Church, Pitsmoor, an early example of a church with charismatic worship in the Church of England. The placement was for six weeks, and the early days proved something of a culture shock, my having never been so close to an evangelical parish community or, of equal importance, worship with charismatic roots.

A task for the placement was to write an essay on ecumenical links—the staff team were keen that I concentrate on the Roman Catholic parish and stay clear of the Methodists and John Vincent (a name that I knew from reading the *Catonsville Roadrunner*, a radical Christian journal, now long gone and forgotten).

I arranged to meet John, and for the rest of the placement I was in regular contact with John, Grace, and the Ashram Community. Those links ensured that I completed the placement, and I'm still in touch with UTU all these years later.

A local newsletter, the *Pitsmoor News*, published a brief piece about me that led to an interview with the *Sheffield Telegraph*, which caused consternation in the parish team, the worry being that I'd been indiscreet about my work with them and their dislike of John—a fear that bore no resemblance to reality.

The opportunity to talk with and learn from John and UTU in those weeks reinforced my commitment to urban ministry and mission that underpinned the next forty-plus years and continues today.

At this stage in the 1970s the importance of urban mission and ministry was not an area of discussion, certainly not an element of the training curriculum of the college course that I was part of, a factor that would seem to be the same today as it was all those years ago.

The creation of the Urban Theology Unit by John Vincent represented an example of an attempt to ensure that the theological and practical issues of urban mission and ministry were addressed. In addition, John had initiated the Sheffield Inner City Ecumenical Mission (SICEM) and the Ashram Community. These three examples of church life rooted in the local community represented innovative initiatives rooted in Christian discipleship.

In Morden, Donald Reeves had created the Urban Mission Project with the intention of training Anglican clergy for urban ministry. In the Church of England there were stirrings of interest among Evangelicals associated with the Mayflower Centre in Canning Town, led by David Sheppard, who would later publish *Built as a City* in 1994; this was predated in 1971 by the creation of the Evangelical Urban Training Project (EUTP), which was another example of the growing if limited interest in urban mission and its importance. This would change with the publication of *Faith in the City* in 1985.

Laying Foundations in Pitsmoor—and Crosscurrents

The six weeks I spent in Pitsmoor were to lay the foundations of my future ministry and establish a friendship with John that would underpin my interest and commitment to urban theological reflection—a key element being to ensure that the local church was committed to working in partnerships both ecumenical and with local public bodies; a lesson learned from John on the importance of mission that looked beyond church buildings.

In the wider context, a close friendship with Ken Leech, which developed from the mid-1970s, brought together two overlapping perspectives on urban mission. John's was rooted in the local community while bringing international perspectives, especially from the United States; through the work of UTU, he enabled creative discussions on every aspect of Christian mission in urban areas. These included the importance of working relationships with local government and the University of Sheffield; through these relationships, he was able with local people to explore the issues and questions of how to create good working relationships between all interested parties.

John's contribution as a New Testament theologian also ensured that insights from biblical theology were paramount in his approach to urban theology. John's views on discipleship were important for me and would influence my ministry. It is important to note that this predates the current interest in the Church of England by over forty years. A key difference between the two approaches is that John was a local practitioner with international experience whose work was rooted in Sheffield, unlike the discussions in the Church of England, which are based on reports from national groupings that seem to have little contact with the everyday reality of ministry in local communities.

Another key element of my weeks in Pitsmoor was the Ashram Community that John and Grace had established. The residents of Ashram House brought together a group of people who contributed to activities in the area and through SICEM. It also was a space where over meals and discussion, ideas and friendship could be developed.

The importance of local communities in this context, which for a period was a key element of the understanding of urban communities, encouraged me to develop my ministry. It laid the foundations for my next forty-five years in ministry, which, apart from an initial three years on a housing estate in Leicester, was a mix of working nationally on urban and social projects for the Church Army or in the London borough Croydon and the Diocese of Southwark.

An interesting contrast with John's approach was that of Ken Leech, who was to become known as a committed urban theologian. While Ken, based in East London, shared John's commitment to the local community, he was skeptical of working with local and national government and was critical of the structures of the Church of England and the leadership of bishops. Ken was a close friend up until his death. His books on urban ministry and theology made an important contribution to Anglican social theology. In addition, his occasional papers and lectures represented a critical contribution to thinking on urban theology and practice, which sadly were of greater influence in the USA than in the Church of England.

While John would serve as president of the Methodist Conference, Ken, even when he worked in the central structures based in Church House Westminster, did not really fit into an institutional structure. His later publications developed his interest in urban theology, and, alongside this interest, his ministry role grew into what was called "community theologian," an original and probably unique role in the Church of England. An important overlap in their theological thinking and ministry were links to the United States and the importance of ensuring that theological reflection underpinned their writing.

Another area of shared interest was the importance of radical Christians working together to promote a critical challenge to the status quo on religious and political questions. Both contributed to the publication *Agenda for Prophets*, a collection of essays edited by Rex Ambler and David Haslam that outlined the potential for a political theology from both a historical and a contemporary perspective, Ken writing on "The Christian Left in Britain (1850–1950)" and John writing on "Doing Theology." The two essays reflect some of their particular interests. The importance of the essays was the attempt to create a political theology for Britain, which sadly had a limited impact, though both John and Ken continued to make important contributions to theological reflection on urban ministry and public issues, rooted in an understanding of what it means to minister to local communities.

In the years following the publication of *Faith in the City*, the importance of urban theology was on the agenda, in a limited sense, of the churches. This was encapsulated in the setting up of the Urban Mission Training Association (UMTA), which brought together representatives of the groups working on the issues and on how mainstream thinking might be influenced; the groups included UTU, Urban Mission Project, Evangelical Urban Training Project, Salford Urban Mission, Urban Presence, the Church Army, and others. However, in retrospect, it had a limited impact apart from its members. UMTA was a loose coalition that encouraged the sharing of ideas and mutual support, which ensured that there was a sense of solidarity. John was a key member of the group and often a catalyst for moving discussions forward.

The importance of urban theology and mission in the Church of England was seen to be important for about ten years after the publication of *Faith in the City* in 1985. This was followed by years where the focus changed; and while a few people like Ken Leech maintained their commitment, they were prophets in a wilderness.

Clash and Paradox

My ministry in urban areas included a secondment to the government's Inner Cities Unit for thirteen months. The intention being that I would be a link between the Church of England and the government in the delivery of their urban policy, the post was not a success in part due to a clash of cultures; the expectation was one of delivery of outputs that failed to recognize the importance of understanding the local community. Measuring delivery without any understanding of the local context was contrary to my understanding, and in following up the analysis of a specific Christian project, I was told to ignore the philosophy that underpinned the report. In this way the fact that the proposal was to bring an employment project to a community of Bengali residents, with the underlying principle of preaching the gospel, was not understood to be a negative approach.

I subsequently worked in Croydon and the Diocese of Southwark on local community projects with a particular interest in public health. For me, in every piece of work, John's model of understanding the community and entering into partnerships with local residents and representatives of the local and health authority was a principle of project development. A key element was also to encourage theological reflection wherever possible.

In my final post prior to retirement, I was the advisor to the bishop for urban life and faith and in a series of meetings with urban clergy from different dioceses was made aware of how the clergy found themselves lacking support, especially in light of the emphasis placed on the report *Mission-Shaped Church*, which seemed to have created an anti-urban approach.[1] The emphasis was on growth in numbers, not the pastoral care of parishioners and the ministry of clergy in deprived urban communities; later developments in many ways followed the government in looking for increased outputs, crudely, bums on pews—a process that fails to take into consideration the everyday reality in local communities.

The contrast with John Vincent and the Methodist Church might not have been very different, though John was able through his seniority in the Methodist Church to ensure that the importance of urban theology and mission was not completely lost from sight, in contrast to the Church of England.

---

1. Church of England Mission and Public Affairs Council, *Mission-Shaped Church*.

In celebrating John's contribution to urban theology and mission, a key element is his staying power, keeping the message relevant, which is highlighted by his personal commitment.

An outcome of my ministry, beginning with my time in Pitsmoor, was a PhD research project with the University of Manchester through Luther King House and, of course, UTU, "Urban Mission and Ministry in the Church of England after *Mission-Shaped Church*," which I started immediately before my retirement—going back to UTU, where my foundations in urban theology had been laid.

Looking back over nearly fifty years in ministry, mainly in urban communities, it is to John that I attribute what followed those days in the spring of 1972. It was his support and friendship that ensured that I was able to continue to the end of my training. The placement in Pitsmoor had the potential to be a disaster, which was paradoxically saved by having to write about an ecumenical project.

Rev. Terry Drummond: Church Army, Anglican deacon, PhD researcher

Bibliography

Ambler, Rex, and David Haslam, eds. *Agenda for Prophets: Towards a Political Theology for Britain*. London: Bowerdean, 1980.

Church of England Mission and Public Affairs Council. *Mission-Shaped Church: Church Planting and Fresh Expressions in a Changing Context*. London: Church House Publishing, 2004.

Sheppard, David. *Built as a City: God and the Urban World Today*. London: Hodder & Stoughton, 1974.

5

Renewing the Church Through Gospel Projects

Geoffrey B. Curtiss

In 1978 I joined an urban ministry course that John Vincent and Ed Kessler were teaching in Philadelphia. I was sent to Philadelphia by my bishop, Jack Spong of Newark. As the curate at Trinity Cathedral in Newark, New Jersey, I was committed to urban ministry, but there were very few options available. Several years earlier, when we were in search for our new bishop, we broke into three groups: rural, urban, suburban; there were fewer than ten people in "urban." In Newark I was searching for ways the church could be relevant to the city. There were five remaining congregations: three on mission status and only two still self-sustaining. We were exploring new ways in which we could work together, and so this course in urban ministry was an opportunity to learn together.

At one afternoon session of the course, John invited us into some self-reflection—one of his great gifts. We were beginning to share our situations and our own perspectives on our work. John and Ed were doing their usual teaching on gospel snaps. But there was some tension because we were being invited to consider some new activities, and our daily calendars were already filled.

John stopped for a moment. He went up to a blank sheet of newsprint and said, "Okay, tell me the things you are currently doing." It started slowly: the upcoming fundraiser; the repair of the electrical system; the relationship with the altar guild; the teen program; and so on. The tension broke as more activities were shared, and some humor surfaced as some of the mundane things we were expected to do joined the list.

"Why are you doing this?" John inquired. After fumbling around for a few minutes, John's typical "I gotcha" moment surfaced. "Now," he asked, "give me a gospel story that explains what you are doing." Whoa . . . a gospel story? Yes. Find a story in the gospel that relates to each of these activities. Slowly but surely we went down the list. People began to connect activities to gospel stories that seemed to fit for them. This one is about hospitality, this one about healing, that about welcoming the young, etc. John kept probing, encouraging, inviting us to see in new ways. Now that we had a gospel action behind what we were doing, we could see how we were not simply inviting people into an activity but into a gospel activity, a way of practicing the gospel. Certainly not all of the listed activities could be linked with a gospel parallel, but the ones that did took on new meaning and new possibility. We could return to our settings and begin to explore Jesus stories that undergirded these activities. Bible study based on activity and practice.

New Meaning and New Questions

Following this course, I returned to Newark with some excitement. During 1979, in downtown Newark, we began a "seminary on the streets" model with three participants using the UTU framework. We had a very successful first year. And out of this experience the Newark Episcopal Cooperative for Ministries was launched among the five Episcopal congregations in Newark.

John had a broader vision and wanted to build a North American network. In 1980 John put together a consultation and invited George Webber, president of New York Theological Seminary, to lead it. There were seventeen participants from New Jersey, New York, Philadelphia, New Orleans. A team of recent participants, including Dr. Al Waller, Mary Lee Talbot, George W. Webber, George Younger, Richard Taylor, Clinton E. Stockwell, Fred B. Williams, John Corcoran, John Vincent, and I, produced a pamphlet entitled *Training for Urban Mission*.[1] We established UTU North America (UTUNA), which held its first meeting at House of Prayer Newark with James Snodgrass as host.

For the next decade Urban Ministry courses were held in Boston, Pittsburgh, Philadelphia, and Hoboken, New Jersey (where I had moved in 1980). John and Ed led an Urban Ministry course in Hoboken from 1981

1. Talbot, *Training for Urban Mission*.

to 1983. At the same time John brought students to New York Theological Seminary from Sheffield for a doctor of ministry course. The students stayed with Linda and me in our new home in Hoboken for their ten-day visit. It was during their visits I first met Ian Duffield and Laurie Green and many other UTU friends from "across the pond."

Several years ago, John asked me to write a piece about UTUNA. In one of the early newsletters, we talked about being an experiential learning and training community delving into the meaning of discipleship and the practices of Jesus. We had about fifty persons on our mailing list, and we sought to be a group of colleagues committed to urban ministry. John often talked about alternative theological education, and many of our participants were engaged in that work through a variety of programs.

Were there alternative ways to be church and resist the denominational structures that suppressed smallness and perpetuated a top-down mentality on congregational life? Through Urban Ministry courses John intended to give special attention to the ways in which local culture, history, political and economic arrangements affect urban ministry and to apply gospel criteria for renewing and reformulating church strategies for city neighborhoods. Of course, as Gibson Winter had so eloquently pointed out, the Protestant churches had been captivated by suburbia, and so he coined the phrase "the suburban captivity of the church."[2] Many cities in the northeastern United States were no longer relevant to the church as they neither provided adequate income for full-time clergy jobs nor paid adequate assessments to denominational structures.

Experiments in Gospel Practice

In Hoboken, I was now located on the eastern front of our diocese. I had been sent to oversee three separate congregations that had not been of any relevance to the diocese since before WWII, providing a wonderful opportunity to practice the methodology of UTU. I was free to try new things, to experiment. The first thing we did was to open a storefront and begin to create gospel projects. Hoboken was a food desert at the time, and the lack of fresh greens, vegetables, cheeses, etc., coalesced a small cadre of people to initiate a food cooperative. The storefront became a hub for community activity. The next gospel project began with addressing the growing crisis caused by the shift in the city's housing policies. Former railroad and dock

2. Winter, *Suburban Captivity*.

workers who had been living in single room occupancy housing (SRO) were now being displaced as a result of the city's decision to disallow SROs as a conforming use. This led me into leading a collaboration between five faith communities and the creation of the Hoboken Shelter for the homeless.[3] The gospel was manifesting itself, and people with little interest in the church were now becoming engaged in ministries of feeding, sheltering, hospitality, and healing—exactly what John had been teaching.

Being around John's energy gave me a number of unique experiences. I was able to join the gatherings in early December at St. Deiniol's Library, spending a week with fellow urban practitioners to explore our individual interests. John's methodology was always to gather our stories and teach from our experience, always bringing the gospel narratives into the center of our discussion. One year he pushed us to bring together our writings and put them together in *Faithfulness in the City*, which he edited. I particularly was moved by conversations with Ann Morisey and Colin Marchant during this week. In the conclusion of the book, John talks about "a new vision for urban living," always bringing it into the contemporary context. What is the new thing we can do? I told the story of my Hoboken experiences of creating new wineskins for the old church facilities. In this highly transitional and gentrifying community I found myself regularly using the "hopes and fears, joys and sorrows" exercise in my Sunday congregation to get at our narrative. The response was amazing. In his usual way again at St. Deiniol's, John challenged us to write, edit our contributions, and use them to present new ways the church was "being the church" in the city.

Growing Networks and Connections

Another experience in 2004 grew out of John's work in New England, a three-day conference with John and Ched Myers dialoguing about the relevance of the Gospel of Mark in today's church and world. John and Ched went back and forth in their own unique ways about how to practice Mark's understanding of discipleship. Ched interpreted Mark into our contemporary political, social, and economic situation, while John testified to the contemporary call to discipleship and what the church needs to imagine as possible.

I was also fortunate to participate in a number of the July gatherings in Sheffield—an opportunity to see UTU in action. We shared in the Sunday

---

3. See https://www.hobokenshelter.org.

morning worship, lived on Abbeyfield Road with people who opened their homes, participated in the new ministries being birthed, for example, turning a pub into a community center. Also, the Ashram Communities and the Roots store demonstrated new expressions of gospel ministries adapting to local contexts. These July visits provided me a time to reflect on my situation, to converse with John and others about what was going on in England around urban ministry. We also had the opportunity to spend time with partners in Sheffield to see and experience new expressions of church. July was always an opportunity to expand my imagination and to consider how others were adapting to a changing and challenging context.

Some important relationships came from my participation with the UTU alumni—for example, my time with Laurie Green and Andrew Davey when their work on urban ministry out of the archbishop of Canterbury's office brought them to New York. Laurie had come to Hoboken in the early eighties with the Sheffield UTU group when he was doing his DMin at New York Theological Seminary. Years later he returned to explore urban ministry, and we spent a wonderful afternoon touring Hoboken and New York. Andrew Davey came to one of our Church and City Conferences to share a global perspective on Urban Mission. Since we all were steeped in the methodology of UTU, we had a common language along with our inquisitive perspectives.

Getting It All Together

I worked alongside John to offer a two-year course called Diploma in Local Church and Community Ministry, and witnessed his continual revising and repurposing of his materials. Often we would gather after the session, and I would discover that John had scratched out on a piece of paper a new idea or reflection that he wanted to share with the group the next day.

In 1998 John presented a wheel diagram of "Getting It All Together." At the center is God, the fire of divine love; the first concentric circle is the ministry of Jesus, and then it blossoms out into a series of three concentric circles of the gospel storehouse, the kingdom of God with spokes directing toward the gospel practices. On one page John diagrammed the essential framework of his hermeneutical method, how the gospel moves in and through the secular world. Another sheet, entitled "Methods and Areas for Gospel Projects," lays out for the participant how we get from situational analysis to "What new way of being church would facilitate your mission or gospel project?" Or "What does our community Gospel Discipleship lead us into?" Or "What does your neighborhood suggest?" Or what could be done by us with these issues now?

John, always future oriented, pushed us to see being church in new ways, to recommit to the ministry of Jesus and forge ahead, to go out into your community and find Jesus practicing already out there ahead of you. Go to Galilee; he is there, not here. This is the Vincent hermeneutical circle, and it was presented in several different ways, depicted in creative images and drawings on a single page, in different exercises in the diploma course or in his writings. Of course, his writings.

In 1998 Elizabeth Kaeton, Carr Holland, Bill Parnell, Laurie Wurm, Harry Smith, and Wayne Holcomb were participants in our diploma course based out of the Diocese of Newark. The mantra for our course became "Every congregation is a gospel project, and every gospel project is a congregation." Elizabeth wrote a piece for our diocesan newsletter entitled "The Full Monty of Urban Theology: Taking It All Off and Putting It All Together." Again the tools of UTU led to exploration of deconstruction and reconstruction, particularly for those who are caught between the status quo of church life with the change and transition happening in their neighborhoods. "Sheffield Inner City Ecumenical Project (SICEM) is a way for small, poor churches in the inner city to carry on, each in their own individual traditions, theology and ways of worship, providing each other encouragement, mutual support, understanding and tolerance."[4] These were her reflections on the ten-day Sheffield experience.

In 2005–6 we ran a course at St. Francis House in New London, Connecticut, that brought together some local folk working with Emmitt Jarrett and Anne Scheibner. One particular project identified working with the homeless and creating a hospitality network. One of the participants, Russ Carmichael, was trying to decide where to locate a center. Through the mapping exercise he discovered that he was looking at the situation backward. Rather than trying to figure out a location from his perspective, he was challenged to map the traveling patterns of homeless folk and find a location centered in their context. At the next session he shared how this exercise had completely changed his perspective on where to locate the center. Rather, he had discovered all the back paths and alternative places they traveled. This led him to develop his gospel project from their perspective rather than from his preconceived notions. During the time we were

---

4. Kaeton, "Full Monty."

in Sheffield for our ten-day visit he created a new proposal for a hospitality center in New London. These are the kind of aha moments or "I gotcha" experiences of the UTU exercises.

You Must First Be a Disciple

For me, John's lecture "Liberation Theology and the Practice of Ministry" given at Queen's College Birmingham captures the essence of his challenge:

> The first implication of liberation theology for the practice of ministry is that location is the decisive first element. The second element is the importance of Situational Analysis: your context determines the questions you should be asking. The third element is to participate in the Prophetic work of the kingdom of God rather than the pastoral work of the church. There is no aspect of human life where God is not seeking now to liberate people from all that oppresses them. The fourth implication is that the Local Christian community itself is the place where the gospel has to be discovered and lived. The fifth implication is the question of a project where non-religious people who join can be kingdom of God people. The implication is you cannot be a minister unless you are first a disciple . . . and discipleship means a total immersion in the character, activity, and destiny of the Lord to whom one is discipled.

John has been an incredible mentor in my life, and his gifts of companionship and willingness to walk alongside me have led me into ministries I would not have conceived of. He helped me understand that smallness is where the gospel is most evident. That throwing seeds without expectations of reaping means success should not be how you measure yourself. Rather, one should recognize that smallness is full of potential and bring together units of gospel projects to share their interests and diversity. I remember the first time I saw the pamphlet on SICEM—I took it and reflected on it, seeking to adapt the concept to my work in Hoboken. Why does the church have to be in one place in the community? Why can it not be in many, networked together? I discovered that ministry was happening in different places, under different roofs, in different neighborhoods. Rather than try to consolidate and unify them, I became interested in celebrating each of them in their own uniqueness. These were gospel projects in their own setting; building partnerships between them became how I adapted the learnings from UTU Sheffield.

John taught out of our experiences. His methods stimulated us to move more deeply into our contexts. For many of us he provided new ways of seeing how small, local congregations could claim a renewed sense of purpose. Rather than lamenting the loss of what once was, he provided gospel pathways into what is and may yet become.

Rev. Geoffrey B. Curtiss: UTU North America tutor, diploma in community ministry

Bibliography

Kaeton, Elizabeth. "The Full Monty of Urban Theology: Taking It All Off and Putting It All Together." *Voice* (Sept. 1998), 4.
Talbot, Mary Lee, ed. *Training for Urban Mission*. Self-published, UTU North America, 1980.
Vincent, John J., ed. *Faithfulness in the City*. New York: Monad, 2003.
Winter, Gibson. *The Suburban Captivity of the Churches*. New York: Doubleday, 1961.

6

Christ in the City in El Salvador

Tony Crisp

As a clinical psychologist who was supervised by John Vincent for a PhD in contextual theology at UTU and ordained to the Roman Catholic diaconate in 2002, I was privileged to spend some time in El Salvador in 2017, when the centenary of the birth of Archbishop Oscar Romero (August 15, 1917) was being celebrated. A group of us spent some time visiting places associated with Romero, but also looking at the work of the church there as it confronts the many and complex social issues in that troubled land. We were staying in the Centro Loyola, which is run by the Central American Province of the Jesuit Fathers. The center is situated in the hills in the southern part of San Salvador, the capital, close to the Universidad Centroamericana (Central American University).[1]

Among my fellow travelers was Father Eamonn O'Brien. I hadn't met Eamonn before. He told me he had spent most of his priestly life teaching in China, in a context very different from my own. One thing we did have in common, however, was that we had both been to Sheffield and both knew John Vincent! An extraordinary coincidence, illustrating quite powerfully the significance and influence of the initiatives John had undertaken

---

1. Situated on the Pacific coast of Central America, El Salvador is about the size of Wales but has twice the population (6.3 million). San Salvador, the capital, is the largest city, with a population of 2.5 million. El Salvador became a sovereign nation in 1841. It has a long history of political and economic instability. Financial corruption in government is a major problem. There is a very high crime rate, particularly gang-related crime and juvenile delinquency. El Salvador has the highest murder rate in the world: 120 homicides per 100,000 inhabitants and rising.

in Sheffield. Eamonn had been to Sheffield some years before I had, but still it was valuable to exchange reminiscences and to reflect upon the ideas of liberation theology and praxis developed in Sheffield and the similarities and differences between the outworking of these and the history and current praxis of the church, particularly the Roman Catholic Church, in El Salvador.

Later during our stay, we went to Divine Providence Hospital, where Archbishop Romero had lived and where in the chapel on March 24, 1980, he had been assassinated. We also visited the Jesuit community house in UCA where "disciples" of Archbishop Romero, Fr. Ignacio Ellacuría, five other Jesuit priests, their housekeeper, and her child had been assassinated in November 1989, and then we met the theologian Fr. Jon Sobrino himself. These were all very moving and unforgettable experiences.

Liberation Theology: Romero and Vincent

As I indicate above, in one of the discussions we had focused on the similarities and differences in praxis between the urban/liberation theology as envisaged and practiced in Sheffield and that of the church in the El Salvadoran context as we were then encountering it. The sociopolitical contexts were significantly different, of course, in so many ways, but there seemed to be two issues in particular that occurred to us, where radically different approaches had been adopted. These issues were not so much of a theological nature as strategic; in particular, the relationship of liberation theology with the church and the relationship between liberation theology and the university.

In his book *The Future of Liberation Theology*, Ivan Petrella has this to say:

> Liberation theology must be wrested from the stranglehold of church and academy. Both church and academy domesticate it by constraining liberation theology within a limited and "proper" definition of theology. Only by releasing itself from this stranglehold can liberation theology's necessarily interdisciplinary nature come forth.[2]

John Vincent quotes this passage with some enthusiasm in *Christ in the City* since it captures one of the defining features of urban theology as he

---

2. Petrella, *Future of Liberation Theology*, 149.

envisages it.³ On "freedom," he writes, "Our independence from denominational and academic control," enables gospel authenticity "to be authentic to the Gospel in a place where the Gospel has not always been heard."⁴ This freedom enabled the foundation of an "alternative theological base" (alternative to an academic setting) to be located in the inner-city of Sheffield, alongside "the people undergoing change in an acute form and the people who live and work with them."⁵ Sheffield, along with other northern cities, had and is still experiencing significant urban deprivation. This base enables different "publics" to be addressed from a new vantage point. Thereby "a context is created in which the academic and missional tasks of the Church look vastly different from what they seemed in the context of university and suburbia, where most church colleges have so far been placed."⁶ From this new perspective, free of institutional constraints, a gospel-based methodology is grounded in "contextual Bible practice," a combination of the "sociocultural analysis of context" with the "sociocultural analysis of Scripture," moving then into action based upon it, in the inner city, to which the label "liberation theology" can be appropriately applied.⁷

Vincent sums up his approach this way: "All liberation theology is contextual, so my theology is a liberation theology based on my context . . . . So I seek to be a disciple in the inner-city and theologise on the basis of it"⁸—in the only theological institution in Britain with outside toilets!⁹

As the above suggests for John Vincent, liberation theology and the UTU in inner-city Sheffield was a deeply personal project to which he has committed much of his life. In a similar way the pastoral praxis of liberation theology, the pursuit of peace with social justice in El Salvador, was a project to which Archbishop Oscar Romero eventually gave his life. However, the origins and development of liberation theology in El Salvador had very different roots.

Before we consider this, a few words about Romero himself. Romero was trained in neo-scholasticism, confrontational in its approach, dogmatic and doctrinaire. Although he was known to be a capable priest, his

---

3. Vincent, *Christ in the City*, 31.
4. Vincent, *Christ in the City*, 22.
5. Vincent, *Christ in the City*, 21.
6. Vincent, *Christ in the City*, 22.
7. Vincent, *Christ in the City*, 28.
8. Vincent, *Christ in the City*, 30.
9. Vincent, *Christ in the City*, 25.

functions were largely administrative. For this reason, some might have said that he was a "priest of the office and the desk." Romero didn't attend Vatican II and gave the outcome a lukewarm response.

Although he became a charismatic and effective preacher, he was yet known for his rigid and demanding attitudes and sometimes provoked animosity among his fellow priests. He was labeled as an obsessive and compulsive perfectionist and somewhat scrupulous. The Medellin conference of the bishops of South and Central America had taken place in 1968, making radical proposals for a new pastoral strategy in the church. The archbishop of San Salvador at that time actively supported these new pastoral approaches, and many priests and pastoral workers were trained in the formation and development of base communities. The formation of base communities within the church, to read, study, and discuss the Bible had the poor and the illiterate at the center of their concern. They had spread rapidly. They built up solidarity among their members, who came to understand that their shared poverty was not the will of God but the consequence of social injustice, which could be prevented.

Because base communities stirred people to action, those in power in the state and in the church perceived them as dangerous, subversive to the status quo, and "communist." Romero was opposed to these developments and attacked the Jesuits for promoting Marxist and liberation theologies. In 1977 Romero was appointed archbishop of San Salvador. He was firmly believed to be a conservative bishop who would resist and reverse the development of base communities and the spread of liberation theology to which the state authorities were absolutely opposed. The killing of priests and pastoral workers known to be involved in the development of base communities had commenced in 1970. On March 12, 1977, just two weeks after he had become archbishop, Fr. Rutillo Grande, his close friend of many years, a seventy-two-year-old parishioner of his, and a twelve-year-old boy were ambushed and killed by the army. This event was to have profound implications for Romero and his understanding of the social and political situation in El Salvador, the consequence being that he would eventually be assassinated himself.

The Conference of Latin American Bishops at their meeting in Medellin, Colombia, produced a set of documents that in effect became the foundational statement of liberation theology in El Salvador. From the beginning the practice of liberation theology was a practice of the church and within the church and in consequence changed the self-understanding of the church itself. Gustavo Gutiérrez in *A Theology of Liberation* writes that the "dualistic" and non-conflictual understanding of the church and the world was superseded at Medellin.[10] Similarly, the theologian José Comblin writes: "We must begin to recognize that the Church was complicit, to a great extent, with underdevelopment and in a special way, with that form of underdevelopment which derives from the American past. All action toward development must begin with a reform of the Church."[11]

A church that no longer sees itself as a *societas perfecta*, standing back from the world, must now take sides. In El Salvador this involved adopting an option in favor of the poor. We see this dramatically manifested in Romero's own life as he moves from being the administrator behind the desk to the pastor among the people.

The establishment of liberation theology, a term chosen by Latin American theologians in the 1960s to indicate a complete break from the past, had necessarily to be accompanied by a liberationist ecclesiology. Base communities in the church became the instrument of this. However, base community is not so much a theological concept as a sociological phenomenon characterized by reciprocity, mutual trust, equality, and shared gospel values operating in a context free from domination and alienation. Liberation theologians have understood base communities as having a political role. Organized groups of the oppressed and the poor facilitate the process of *concientización*, which awakens them to the nature of the oppression that so dominates their lives. As they reflect upon the Bible in the context of their lives and act upon the judgments made, so their faith is manifested politically. Thousands of base communities were established in Latin America following the Medellin conference. We were introduced to some in El Salvador. I will describe what we found below.

An Alternative Pedagogy

The Medellin documents gave particular attention to education and in doing so was profoundly influenced by the work of Paulo Freire. *Liberating education* as Freire uses the term transforms the student into the subject of her own development. Education is key to liberating the masses from oppression. These ideas are taken up by Ignacio Ellacuría, who was strongly influenced by Oscar Romero in the context of university education.

---

10. Gutiérrez, *Liberation Theology*, 41.
11. Comblin, "Ecclesiologies of Medellin," 68.

Ellacuría was rector of Central American University in San Salvador. In a book entitled *Toward a Society That Serves Its People*, we find his paper entitled "Is a Different Kind of University Possible?" Here, he asks the question "What is the fundamental mission or purpose of a university?" and then outlines a new vision for university education, which he proceeds to implement in Central American University. This new vision has several elements to it. First a university must move away from a pedagogy that seeks primarily the passive transmission of knowledge, toward an "active emphasis on socio-historical change in favour of the equality and justice required for overcoming oppression and moving forward toward a fuller realization of human dignity."[12] Such a university then, in its engagement with society, commits itself to opposing injustice and creating a new society in which the poor and the marginalized are at the center of its concern.

Ellacuría calls the fundamental stance of such a university *social projection*. Social projection is a two-way process. On the one hand, it involves the university recognizing its responsibility to insert itself into society, using its resources of knowledge, research, and teaching for purposes of social transformation. On the other hand, the university allows the real problems of society to profoundly influence the way it functions in terms of its administration, its teaching curriculum, and its research priorities. The university then is alert to and engaged with the real social-historical context in which it exists—in a dynamic relationship with it.

It is not possible to do justice to the depth and complexity of Ellacuría's thinking here. However, he and other theologians in El Salvador saw the university, alongside the church, as having a fundamental role to play in the social transformation they sought to pursue.

During our visit to El Salvador, we were enabled to experience the church and university in action. For example, the Centro Loyola functioned in a similar way to the center in Abbeyfield Road in Sheffield. It used its resources, residential, library, and conference facilities to reach out into the community so as to support the work of base communities in the city. Considerable attention is given to enabling group members to understand government policies and procedures and how they impact upon their lives, how to lobby politicians and government officials, to assert their rights and seek change.[13] Particular consideration is given to women's participation

---

12. See Gandolfo, "Different Kind of University," 162.

13. While we were there, there was a major dispute growing over water privatization and its impact upon the poor.

in the life of communities. Many women are on their own since their husbands have traveled to America or are gang members and have abandoned them. Helping women to know their rights, develop self-esteem, and become leaders in their communities is an important objective. Women are becoming increasingly active in forming small businesses, e.g., bakeries, to promote the growth of family income and savings. The church is actively concerned with promoting personal health. Counseling is provided for those traumatized by violence, which is a serious problem given the level of violence in the city. Workshops on the development of respectful relationships are offered.

In the city at large the church is actively involved in promoting peace between rival gangs. The church is trusted in a way that the government is not since the government relies exclusively upon the police and the army to confront the gangs. In 2012 the church brokered a major truce between two rival gangs, which significantly reduced the homicide rate in the city at that time.

We were taken to meet a base community in a part of the city controlled by gangs. They had converted part of the church premises into a sports facility and encouraged members of gangs to compete with each other rather than fight each other. A football match was taking place while we were there. This is very dangerous work. Situations can deteriorate very rapidly.

The church is very active in changing the culture within schools, where most gang members are recruited. The church is promoting a culture of cooperation rather than competition, peace education and gender and cultural sensitivity. Similar work is going on in base communities and parishes. Some schools have been established on the boundaries between gang territories, encouraging the forming of friendship between families and children of gang members. We were hoping to visit one of these schools but were advised that this would not be possible at that time as the situation was "tense."

The church is also involved in promoting human rights and justice by providing legal aid and investigative resources, counseling for the poor and others who have been subject to human rights abuses.

On visiting Central American University, it was very evident that Ellacuría's ideas had had a significant impact upon its way of life. Ellacuría's memory was highly respected there. A shrine was dedicated to him, close to the place where he was assassinated. I witnessed many students making their way to the shrine on their way to classes. Many if not most classes were held in the evening; the majority of students worked in the city during the day. This was a manifestation of the idea of social projection that was at the heart of Ellacuría's thinking. The students brought their experience of society, work, and city life into the university, and in turn through the university curriculum the students were enabled to reflect theologically, philosophically, and social-scientifically on their experience and their context, *conscientización* (raising of consciousness), and then return into society with a new sensitivity/understanding of their personal and social situation and the oppressive forces at work within it.

It was clear that over the years since 1968 the church and the university had been increasingly agents of radical change (liberation) in El Salvador. This was not because of the influence of marginal members on the fringe of the church as was the case in other countries of South and Central America, but because the leaders of the church and university had committed themselves to this agenda, at great personal cost to themselves.

During our visit to the university, we met Martha Zechmeister, CJ. She is professor of systematic theology in the university and had been a pupil of Johann Baptist Metz in Germany. She reminded us of Metz's definition of Christian mysticism as "mysticism with open eyes." Metz had been influenced by the Jewish philosopher Hans Jonas, who had written, "See and you will know." In one of her unpublished papers, Zechmeister has written:

> The Christian experience of the Gospel has nothing to do with shutting our senses to the external world, but rather with an awakening, an awakening from our dreams and fantasies into the real world, created and loved by God and yet at the same time a world which has been perverted and disfigured by scandalously unjust distribution, in which millions of people are starving, are confronted by deadly violence and ultimately brutal deaths.[14]

Our visit to El Salvador opened our eyes to the "real," the brutality of life there. What we witnessed in El Salvador, the reality of life there, is so very different from the urban deprivation we may encounter in Sheffield, but our response should be the same: seeing and judging and then acting, that is, "walking together with my fellow men and women and together with my wounded brothers and sisters who become companions and guides on the way to the mystery of God" (oral quote from Zechmeister).

---

14. Zechmeister, "Passion for God," unnumbered page.

Rev. Dr. Tony Crisp: Roman Catholic deacon, clinical psychologist, UTU PhD graduate, PhD supervisor

Bibliography

Comblin, José. "Cristianismo y dissarrollo." In *La historia crisrianismo en America Latina*, edited by Hans-Jürgen Prien, 462–82. Salamanca: Sigueme, 1985.

———. "The Ecclesiologies of Medellin and the Lessons of Base Communities." Translated by William Cavanaugh. *Cross Currents* 44 (1994), 67–84.

Ellacuría, Ignacio. "Is a Different Kind of University Possible?" In *Toward a Society That Serves Its People*: The *Intellectual Contribution of El Salvador's Murdered Jesuits*, edited by John Hassett and Hugh Lacey, 177–207. Washington, DC: Georgetown University Press, 1991.

Gandolfo, David I. "A Different Kind of University Within the University: Ellacuría's Model in the Context of the United States." In *A Grammar of Justice: The Legacy of Ignacio Ellacuría Today*, edited by J. Matthew Ashley et al., 161–72. Maryknoll, NY: Orbis, 2014.

Gutiérrez, Gustavo. *A Theology of Liberation*. Maryknoll, NY: Orbis, 1988.

Petrella, Ivan. *The Future of Liberation Theology: An Argument and Manifesto*. Burlington, VT: Ashgate, 2004.

Sobrino, Jon. "Monseñor Romero's Impact on Ignacio Ellacuría." In *A Grammar of Justice: The Legacy of Ignacio Ellacuría*, edited by J. Matthew Ashley et al., 57–76. Maryknoll, NY: Orbis, 2014.

Vincent, John J. *Christ in the City: The Dynamics of Christ in Urban Theological Practice*. Sheffield: UTU, 2013.

Zechmeister, Martha. "Passion for God." Unpublished manuscript, 2015. Photocopy.

PART III

The Primacy of Discipleship

Introduction

Orientation to the Primacy of Discipleship

Ian K. Duffield

John talks about a journey downward, alongside, backward, and sideways.[1] This fundamental challenge to how one lives contrasts with the journey upward, which is the default position for most people. This alternative journey is essentially about discipleship, which was the focus of his doctorate in Switzerland and continued to be John's preeminent concern. In some ways, discipleship is a form of vocation. So, not surprisingly, John would run courses on vocation, helping young people discern their vocation—their task, their role in life. In the study year, this became a year-long enterprise in which he would challenge them to see the city as the location for their vocation through immersing them in the urban realities alongside sessions on Mark's Gospel and so on. This was modeled on a pattern of discipleship where "feet" came first and "head" last. In this way, many people's lives were changed and given a trajectory, whether they called it discipleship explicitly or not.[2]

In many ways, discipleship helps to link the primacies. So, discipleship, as understood through the Gospel of Mark, characterizes John's approach and explains his continuing appeal to people to embrace urban discipleship. Such discipleship is inherently contextual. It's about being a disciple in a particular situation, at a particular point of time. And such discipleship is about an outworking of the gospel within contemporary secular reality, which will often lead to a practice that may be seen as within or reflective of

1. Vincent, *Alternative Journeys*.
2. On the relation between location and vocation, see Duffield, "Urban Theology."

the radical Christian tradition. John, of course, has exemplified this in his own life by his radical discipleship in a poor part of Sheffield.

Recently, my church, the Church of England, has started advocating discipleship, but, unfortunately, it is light-years away from John's approach if only because it is an institutional imposition in hock to a church growth strategy rather than an invitation to change one's life, to journey downward, to be alongside the poor.

As is evident in his doctorate, John's focus on discipleship is rooted in his understanding of Mark's Gospel, and he frequently uses study of that gospel to engage folk with the demands of discipleship. So, Mark's Gospel becomes naturally the next primacy.

Bibliography

Duffield, Ian K. "Urban Theology: Location, Vocation, and Action." In *Faithfulness in the City*, edited by John J. Vincent, 266–79. New York: Monad, 2003.

Vincent, John J. *Alternative Journeys: Gospel Calls for the Eighties*. Sheffield: UTU, 1981.

7

Journey with John: Disciple, Scholar, and Friend

Nirmal Fernando

I HAVE BEEN ASKED to write about the mutual relationship between me and John, one who is not only a recognized theologian in the academy, but more importantly continues to live out that theology, which he has consistently done in day-to-day life, perhaps from even before I was born.

It was in the summer of 2008 that we first met. I had written an essay on "Kingdom of God and Church," which John had read. He invited me to come to Sheffield to take things further, and so he was there at the Sheffield Interchange to pick me up. With Grace driving and John talking, he said that my essay must be published in the next *ACT Together*, the biannual journal of the Ashram Community. John said, one brings a useful gift, we show appreciation and make use of it. To me that could be likened to the sharing of the disciples of Jesus as expressly described in Acts 2 and 4. Hence, John's welcome was not just a smile and a handshake but an acceptance and appreciation.

John, being one who had an interest in other cultures and religious traditions, initially asked that I start an interfaith project at Burngreave Ashram. Consequently, in that very same year, later in the summer, we launched the Multifaith Chapel and Library. It was at the opening of that space welcoming those of all faiths and none that John introduced me to the UTU, by bringing along those at the UTU Summer School to the opening event.

From that time onward, over the many years to follow until the autumn of 2019, it was a journey with John, as disciple, student, researcher, writer, and friend, whether in Sheffield where I was half a month, in London where I spent the other half, or on holiday in Sri Lanka, my land of birth.

The Call of Discipleship

John is not about converting people to Christianity. He is about calling people to live out discipleship as depicted in the narratives about Jesus. Further, he is always aware of the duty cast upon one who has seriously committed to discipleship to carry on the lineage by selecting disciples to be with him and to go out in mission (see Mark 3:13–14); those indeed, were rightly John's disciples in Jesus, and so, I am privileged to be one among them.

To John, discipleship had to be intentional. Interpreting the Greek μετανοεῖτε in Mark 1:15 as "looking aside," he consistently stressed the importance of doing that intentionally; to intentionally follow the intentional invitation of the one who calls. John always did that with discernment, by personally calling from one individual to the next as they cross his path in life. To me, in reception, it was a call to look away from all extant mainstream cultures of the day—conventional, popular, or other, a change of mind and way of life, to become part of a benign alternative culture.

John's call to discipleship was a repetition of that of Jesus; a call to follow the way of life of the kingdom of God, which to him is the εὐαγγέλιον (one gospel). Accordingly, he was about creating intentional communities here and there in England, whenever there were two or three who will gather together in Jesus's name (Matt 18:20), to try to live out the kingdom in discipleship. If John is asked if the UTU is such an intentional community, it is extremely doubtful if he'll reply in the negative.

Like Jesus, John selected home bases for discipleship community life. Some were houses where people lived caringly, sharing together, and others were homes of individuals and families that hosted discipleship gatherings from time to time. Further, John was always an advocate of accepting those made vulnerable in society in disciple community houses. To me, that was a new experience and a process of learning, particularly the virtue of tolerance, by living with refugees, those impoverished, alcoholics, and transsexuals. That was indeed a blessing to me.

As Student of John

Like Jesus, John is a teacher, and he taught me without counting cost or seeking any reward. Sometimes this was one to one and at other times in groups. Apart from numerous other study sessions he conducted, we carefully studied the entire New Testament over time. Also, we systematically read together and discussed his doctoral dissertation on "Discipleship in Mark," completed in 1960 at the renowned Basel University in Switzerland, supervised by the well-known ecumenist and theologian Professor Oscar Cullmann and examined by the legendary Karl Barth, who strongly disagreed with John's views but asked that he not change a word of the thesis. Thereafter, John wrote and published *Secular Christ* in 1968, which as I know was read and used in many parts of the world. Subsequently, we also studied that with John explaining and humbly criticizing his own work, like he did when we studied his doctoral work, some fifty years after he wrote it.

Perhaps that which was most important to me was his teaching of biblical Greek. Like a prayer, each and every week, at the agreed time, John came down to our community home at Rock Street in Sheffield, Greek Testament in hand, to teach a handful of us the language of Jesus's recorded words, without which, as I soon realized, it is impossible for me to rightly understand Jesus.

My inquisitive attitude, not just accepting things but wanting to get to the bottom of all things, including that which is religious, was well nourished by John. Hence, whenever I asked him questions, or where I could find resources about one or another aspect connected with Jesus or theology, his long experience and wide knowledge on the subject enabled him not only to often give immediate satisfactory answers but also to refer me to the source material. Further, it was not uncommon for John to say he has that book and would bring it along the next day or to say, "You'll find that at the UTU." Once John got me going on that line, I would find useful resources on websites and information on new publications, which I used to print out or order and share together with John, as relevant at group sessions. Systematic biblical research was introduced and taught to me by John; something which I have now developed and continue from day to day, often giving thanks and praise for the solid foundation laid by him.

True Friendship

John never calls me "friend"—he speaks to me by my name in public, but often calls me "old son" one-on-one. However, he referred to me as "friend" when writing for one of his books, also saying that I had "lovingly carried out" what I was asked to do. True friendship with selfless love, doing what one is asked to do, after all, as Jesus said, is how his disciples are recognized. I recall: "You are my friends if you do what I tell you" (John 15:14) and "By this everyone will know that you are my disciples—if you have ἀγάπην (selfless love) for one another" (John 13:35).

True to being John's disciple, student, researcher, writer, and friend, I always try to live up to that, even though we are now some 5,500 miles away as the crow flies. John continues in community in UTU and Ashram in England, while I do the same among these simple villagers who are a natural community of carers and sharers, extending unreserved hospitality in a remote rural location in Sri Lanka, quite off the beaten track.

Nirmal Fernando: interfaith project worker at Burngreave Ashram, originally from Sri Lanka

8

Discipleship, Context, and Lived Religion

James Curry

I FIRST MET JOHN when I joined the MPhil/PhD group at UTU in 2009. As we spoke, I found out that he had known two of the most influential figures in my life, George MacLeod, the founder of the Iona Community, and David Jenkins, a former bishop of Durham. I took this as a good omen that we would get on well together—which we did! I arrived at UTU with a rather vague proposal of investigating a phenomenon sometimes called "churchless Christianity." John and I spoke at length about this, and after a few sessions he looked at me with what I later knew to be his characteristic shrewdness and asked: "Are there really so many churchless Christians in your area?"—which forced me to think again! John then encouraged me to explore widely around the subject and to see what related ideas might be worth looking into. This led to my researching such areas as intentional communities and how people learn about their faith and proved very useful in providing me with an overview of my subject area. Then, given his passion and expertise in this, it was no surprise that John advised me to explore my particular context in detail in order to find out what was really going on there, socially and theologically. In doing so, I was inspired by John's own definition of what contextual theology involves: a *contextual theology* sets out a version of Christian faith, discipleship, and philosophy produced by the practice of specific Christians and their reflection on that practice, within a certain historical, social, cultural, political, and class situation.[1] I found the exploration of my context one of the most stimulating

---

1. Duffield et al., *Crucibles*, 24.

aspects of the research process, and John was keen for me to tease out what was distinctive and particular for the practice of theology for those living within my context.

After I had explored my context in detail, John then encouraged me to reflect on what I had discovered, especially in terms of the theological implications of what I had found and what this revealed about people and their Christian discipleship—conceivably, John's hallmark theological theme throughout his many years of preaching and teaching. His emphasis on the importance of discipleship helped me to see its relevance to my own research. John's words reveal the passion that has sustained him for so long. In an article for members of his own intentional community, the Ashram Community, John wrote:

> To me, Discipleship is always primary . . . Discipleship means being a disciple—in our case, a disciple of Jesus Christ. . . . Once you have opted for Jesus as his disciples he leads you into mysteries about what he is doing and he is opening up. So, a constant search for the reality of the Master is an essential part of Discipleship. . . . [Then] we cement our discipleship with real, tangible, durable practice done together.[2]

Elsewhere, John expanded upon what contemporary discipleship involves by identifying what he terms "the great questions of discipleship," and these include:

- What to be
- Who to be
- How to be
- Whose to be
- Where to be
- With whom to be
- What to do

All down through history, Christians have been would-be disciples, have seen themselves as trying to be contemporary followers. So, what might that mean for us today?

---

2. Vincent, "Ashram."

> How can we be "followers" of Jesus? What issues that we have today can get help from [the gospel] stories? How can we as disciples today get together our own lives in the light of [our Christian] tradition? What might it mean for each one of us, personally and together, to follow this way—or even just bits of it?[3]

These additional questions helped to crystallize what I was discovering as important elements in my own research.

Perhaps above all, I am indebted to John for enabling me to see my research as an unfolding journey, where key ideas and deeply held convictions within my situation were gradually revealed and it became possible to discern what aspects of people's faith truly mattered to them. In practical terms, what this meant was that my research subject developed from a focus on churchless Christianity, through an exploration of personal spirituality, and ended with a detailed investigation of lived religion, the topic that emerged from the process of contextual analysis and theological reflection that John had been instrumental in guiding me toward.

This has been very much a personal appreciation of the way John has helped me as a research student. Others will undoubtedly be able to write more knowledgeably of his extensive biblical scholarship and his major contribution to urban theology. But finally, I would like to pay tribute to John as a pastor. At one point during my time at UTU I was under considerable pressure professionally. John listened to me carefully and compassionately and gave me excellent counsel for which I shall always be grateful. So, thank you, John, for all your help, guidance, and support, as a supervisor, teacher, and friend—and for the record, you have now joined those who have influenced my thinking and ministry. It is a privilege to know you.

Rev. Dr. James Curry: Anglican priest, PhD graduate

Bibliography

Duffield, Ian K., et al. *Crucibles: Creating Theology at UTU*. New City Special 14. Sheffield: UTU, 2000.
Ingham, Howard M., et al., eds. *Reading the Bible: Approaching and Understanding Scripture*. Birmingham, UK: Student Christian Movement, 2006.
Vincent, John. "Ashram: Discipleship, Community and Projects." *Act Together* 79 (2015), 16. http://www.ashram.org.uk/Act%20Together%20Spring%202015A.pdf.

---

3. John Vincent, in Ingham et al., *Reading the Bible*, 2.

9

John Vincent's Alternative Church

Christine Dutton

IN THE AUTUMN OF 2008, I sat with the new Urban Theology Unit PhD students in the front room of Abbeyfield Road as we began to sketch out our research proposals to one another and the staff. Rather intimidated by the forensic interrogation of John Vincent, Ian K. Duffield, Robin Pagan, and Paul Walker, I am not sure I slept much that night, rather unsure of what I was letting myself in for. The next morning, John strode down the hill and said he hadn't slept much either—he was busy thinking over all our first stumbling efforts to bring our own learning and contexts into what would be theological and ecclesiological frameworks from which to draw conclusions. We had come with our hunches and problematics (as I came to understand the language of UTU) and had on hand a group of like-minded, passionate, and rigorous scholars ready to help us shape and form these ideas into coherent arguments. During my studies at UTU, I candidated as a Methodist presbyter and for a number of years combined my doctoral studies in Sheffield with ministerial training at Hartley Victoria College based at Luther King House, cementing relationships that would be strengthened as the validation for UTU's doctoral program moved from Birmingham University to Manchester in 2014.

Beginning with Joys and Sorrows

This was the beginning of my journeying with John, and throughout my doctoral research, his interest never waned, he always had another insight, another book to read, another nugget of Mark's Gospel to include, offered with generosity and encouragement. After UTU moved to Victoria Hall the hospitality that he and Grace offered at their home was warmly welcome. His sharp prophetic insight is rooted in his love for Methodism. One of the key elements of the PhD seminar group that gathers students together for intensive learning and peer review is that each session always begins with orientation. John had instituted this for the DMin back in the late 1970s, and it continues to this day with researchers, book writers, and supervisors sharing with each other. This extensive period of listening and learning as each participant "shares joys and sorrows" (one of John's creative strategies that has been a feature of the way he works with people), new insights, or experiences is a strategy I have intentionally used in circuit ministry: at the beginning of meetings, small groups, and often tweaked for informal worship. Time spent engaged in orientation always produces a deeper level of engagement and attention to the subsequent task in hand.

John's writings have also been influential for my research and ministry and my engagement with contemporary ecclesiology in the Methodist Church. John's desire for any new incarnations or reinventions of church to be grassroots communities are gospel focused—driven by the desire to encourage others to follow the Jesus way, interpreting their discipleship by close engagement with their communities. Writing this, while *O.K., Let's Be Methodists* is never far from my desk, it is John's 1976 volume *Alternative Church* that almost fifty years later I want to bring into dialogue with the trajectory or rather cyclical understanding of the church's constant reinventing of itself, particularly with regards to the journey the Methodist Church has taken over the last twenty years through its engagement with the ecumenical Fresh Expressions movement to the current God for All strategy.

The strategy accepted by Methodist Conference in 2020 puts discipleship at its heart, embracing a Methodist way of life introduced by Roger Walton and encouraging all disciples to embrace twelve elements that illustrate what it means to be a follower of Jesus today. Taking seriously areas of the outworkings of faith: worship, learning, caring, service and evangelism—the God for All strategy requires any new way of "doing church differently" not simply to repackage and deliver any one model of church but to intentionally build community that has discipleship at its core.

"Doing church differently" was terminology I deliberately fashioned for use in my thesis. Having wrestled with decades of language attempting to define experiments in new ways of being church, I wanted a more neutral form of wording. From my own fieldwork researching Methodist Fresh Expressions (2010–12), as well as having led and participated in many examples subsequently, the offer of learning and deepening discipleship has always been one of its key hallmarks, and it has supported and nurtured those who have attended worship gatherings.

John's practice and observation of para-churches of the 1960s and 1970s drew deeply on his understanding of Leonardo Boff's basic Christian communities.[1] The illustrations in *Alternative Church* were local expressions of grassroots communities, often ecumenical in their nature, led by "more or less committed members of institutional churches" who identified gaps or needs unfulfilled by their denominations.[2] Their involvement in the foundation and leadership of such para-churches was seen as "alongside" their committed engagement in traditional forms of local churches. This was observed to be the case for lay and ordained alike.

As the new millennium turned, traditional denominations were wrestling with their identity. The membership of the Methodist Church had declined dramatically, yet para-church experiments such as John's in the 1970s had continued to flourish alongside and as part of many traditional churches. The Church of England published its *Mission-Shaped Church* report identifying and categorizing way of "doing church differently,"[3] and Rowan Williams introduced the language of "mixed economy."[4] There was a return to the same questions that John had highlighted thirty years previously—but whereas *Alternative Church*, to my mind, is full of experimentation and hope, soon the need of the institution of the Church of England to measure growth and be accountable for finance heralded a rhetoric of fresh expressions as the salvation of the church. This is witnessed in the subsequent report *From Anecdote to Evidence*, based on research undertaken from 2011 to 2013.[5] The summary of the research implied a far greater "success" drawn from a relatively small sample and thus ran the risk of extrapolating a trajectory for a denomination from what were joyful local glimpses of contextual yet fragile emerging and alternative church

---

1. See Boff, *Ecclesiogenesis*.
2. Vincent, *Alternative Church*, 14.
3. Church of England Mission and Public Affairs Council, *Mission-Shaped Church*.
4. Williams, "Archbishop's Presidential Address," para. 12.
5. Church Growth Research Programme et al., *From Anecdote to Evidence*.

experiments. Closer evaluation and analysis of "doing church differently" is explored in my thesis.[6]

In the Church of England, an additional pioneer training pathway for ordained priests was created; new church plants emerged that were under Bishop's Mission orders. These new congregations could claim John's title "para-church" but appeared to erode the parish system—seemingly disregarding clergy and congregations who had for decades been working with local communities, proclaiming the gospel afresh in every generation through the slow burn of incarnational presence and building trust and relationships in both rural and urban settings.

In the Methodist Church, VentureFX was created. Funding for the initiative released both lay and ordained pioneers at connexional level, and a small number of creative experiments in building and forming communities emerged. But this initiative (designed for a ten-year period from 2009 onward) and the Anglican pioneer pathway were only ever going to have a limited impact.

The potential for substantial grassroots change, as John suggested, began to happen as the Methodist Church formally partnered with the Church of England in the Fresh Expressions initiative. Energy was released and training provided to help congregations to take seriously the context and ecclesial landscape they found themselves in and to think about their own specific location in which they might "do church differently." The language itself, though problematic, held the hope and intention that with support from the Fresh Expressions initiative, new communities and churches might be planted and nurtured, specifically aimed at those without any prior connection to churches.

In its cyclical nature, as experiments run their natural course, are reinvented, renamed, as personnel come and go, funding dries up. Sometimes what begins at the edge moves toward the center. This can be seen in the example of Somewhere Else, the bread church that began in 1999 following the closure of Liverpool's Methodist Central Hall to a city center post without a church building. The subsequent formation of a community of bread makers, who shared each others' lives, held each others' stories, and developed into a community who then prayed and studied Scripture together held many of the hallmarks of the alternative church. Never imagining itself as the "answer" to the church's problems, they lived fairly precariously, trusting that each day they met, God would reveal to them a small glimpse

---

6. See Dutton, "Ecclesial Reality."

of the realm of God. As people heard the story of the bread church and read Barbara Glasson's accounts of the community, people came and saw, and then took the idea away and adapted bread making for their own contexts.[7]

There is a sense in which the organic and grassroots communities hold the fragility yet the boldness of the first disciples as they take risks in following Jesus. Communities I have had the privilege of being part of demonstrate that when new followers come, they are eager to learn more. Jesus did this in a structured way, with a manageable number, and John Wesley replicated this wisdom as he created his "class system." It was here in the safety and companionship of others who sought to follow Jesus that learning took place, not simply receiving teaching but actively participating and being nurtured in risk-taking discipleship. In a time when traditional engagement in learning outside of a Sunday for prayer and studying Scripture seems to be waning, new communities that are setting up are finding that access to online provision is making the creation of discipleship groups possible in a new and accessible way. Wayne Grewcock in the Exeter District brought together four Methodist Churches during the COVID-19 lockdown of 2020 for online Sunday worship. When three out of the four communities returned to worship in buildings, Shoreline continued to provide online Sunday worship for those who had joined them during lockdown—they were no longer geographically based and included those who had joined the online community. Recognizing the need to foster ongoing learning and engagement, a weekly discipleship and study session has been added to the Sunday worship for those who want to learn more about the Christian faith together. The Urban Theology Unit has also benefited from online discipleship opportunities by gathering those geographically dispersed to consider the recently published Kingdom Evangelism resources.

Returning to the experiments of the 1970s, the great gift of *Alternative Church* was John's declaration that the position of para-churches (read Fresh Expressions, New Places for New People, etc.) by virtue of being "alongside the denominations and the ecumenical church" thus "purposely retains this ambiguous but strategic position."[8] John recognized that these alternative expressions were "for some . . . the only possible Church."[9] Those church communities and denominations that have taken risks in offering alternative worship and small groups at times and in places that respond to

---

7. Glasson, *I Am Somewhere Else*; *Mixed-Up Blessing*.
8. Vincent, *Alternative Church*, 105.
9. Vincent, *Alternative Church*, 106.

rapidly changing working and family patterns have continued to adapt and grow even in the face of declining traditional worship attendance in the mainstream denominations.

When I was writing my thesis, reflecting on Methodist Fresh Expressions, despite wrestling with the dissonance often between the rhetoric of the denominations and the reality of the grassroots expressions, I never lost sight of John's rallying cry at the end of *Alternative Church*: "The Para Church must happen. Tired Christians Need It. Modern Society Needs It. Estranged People Need It. The Gospel Needs It."[10]

Now having moved to the Queen's Foundation in Birmingham, I worship frequently at Inclusive Gathering Birmingham. Sitting lightly to definitions and labels, this fragile community supported by the Methodist Church meets in borrowed rooms, online, and in cafés and homes around the city. It draws those who have been rejected and estranged by the traditional church as well as those who are tired and seeks to offer an alternative that does not replace but to my mind holds the "ambiguous but strategic position" of holding up to the church a reminder of what we can be when, alongside the many gifts of our tradition, we open ourselves up to learning to experiment with the new, so that we continually become a place of welcome and hospitality for all who are searching for the hope of Christ and his alternative and revolutionary way of peace and love.

I am grateful to John for his wisdom, his challenge, his colleagueship, his generosity, and his encouragement over my time as a student and tutor at UTU. May his vision of an alternative church that nurtures and embodies discipleship continue to remain a reality for the sake of the gospel.

Rev. Dr. Christine Dutton: PhD graduate; PhD supervisor; tutor in evangelism and leadership at Queen's Foundation, Birmingham

Bibliography

Church of England Mission and Public Affairs Council. *Mission-Shaped Church: Church Planting and Fresh Expressions in a Changing Context*. London: Church House Publishing, 2004.

Boff, Leonardo. *Ecclesiogenesis: The Base Communities Reinvent the Church*. Maryknoll, NY: Orbis, 1986.

10. Vincent, *Alternative Church*, 133.

Church Growth Research Programme, et al. *From Anecdote to Evidence: Findings from the Church Growth Research Programme 2011–2013*. N.p.: Church Commissioners for England, 2014. https://www.churchofengland.org/sites/default/files/2019-06/from_anecdote_to_evidence_-_the_report.pdf.

Dutton, Christine Margaret. "The Ecclesial Reality of Fresh Expressions: 'Doing Church Differently' in the Liverpool District of the Methodist Church." PhD diss., University of Birmingham, 2017. https://etheses.bham.ac.uk//id/eprint/7885.

Glasson, Barbara. *I Am Somewhere Else: Gospel Reflections from an Emerging Church*. London: Darton, Longman and Todd, 2006.

———. *Mixed-Up Blessing: A New Encounter with Being Church*. Peterborough, UK: Inspire, 2006.

Vincent, John J. *Alternative Church*. Belfast: Christian Journals, 1976.

Williams, Rowan. "Archbishop's Presidential Address—General Synod, York, July 2003." Dr Rowan Williams, July 14, 2003. http://rowanwilliams.archbishopofcanterbury.org/articles.php/1826/archbishops-presidential-address-general-synod-york-july-2003.html.

PART IV

The Primacy of Mark's Gospel

Introduction

Orientation to the Primacy of Mark's Gospel

Ian K. Duffield

For John, it is primarily the Gospel of Mark (and particularly the first eight chapters, and certainly not the Old Testament or St. Paul) that provides him with his exclusive canon within the canon—his touchstone for his understanding of Christianity. In many ways this is the central primacy from which the others emanate.

John sees Mark as the most secular of the gospels (hence he can talk of a "secular Christ"), as teaching is at a minimum and the stress is on action in this gospel and, hence, most conducive to an urban reading and the stress on practice. And it is through Mark that John discerns the realities of "discipleship" and a radical Jesus who requires a personal and corporate response. It's there in his doctorate, writings, and throughout his ministry. Each year, it seems, he has worked through Mark with others investigating what he calls "the dynamics of Christ."[1] As we have seen, that dynamic focuses on the primacies of discipleship and practice (below). But a discipleship rooted in the secular (hence: secular Christ); and of course that means the urban, the city, or more precisely, the inner city, for John, hence urban Christ. For him personally it means Burngreave and the Pitsmoor area of Sheffield where he was the Methodist minister for most of his career and where he still lives and worships.

John posits a correlation between Mark's narrative of Jesus's activity in Galilee with the secular world and sees in the former the archetype of gospel activity and the key antecedent for Christian practice today. John

1. Vincent, *Christ in the City*, 2.

Introduction to Part IV

envisions, thereby, a "secular Christ" and an "urban Christ," connecting the past with the present, and in this way dissolving the historical/cultural gap that prevents so many from discovering the practical relevance of the text for today, as they think the gap cannot be bridged. Alternatively, others bridge the gap far too quickly, as if it's possible to read off simplistically what action in the present is required in our totally different, secular world. With prophetic imagination the gap can be bridged and action released, but this is not superficial or surface repetition or a fundamentalist move that is decontextual, but rather a creative engagement between then and now, between the text in its context and ourselves in our current context. So, snap is followed by study in the sequence he advocates (see below), and that study includes both situation analysis and gospel practice analysis. It's a discovering of a "correspondence" of relationship between them; it is a current inhabiting of the "dynamics of Christ" so that gospel action happens again.[2]

Not surprisingly, in the kind of gospel analysis that John argues for, it is from Mark that he finds the "Marks," i.e., "Marks of the Gospel" (an identification exercise that has often been undertaken at UTU with different groups of people), indications and intimations and insights into how one may discern the gospel acting today within the secular, the urban, the city. And John works closely with the text to identify those marks in an interactive way. In *Mark at Work*, John and John D. Davies proposed a simple but effective strategy for this: snap, study, spin-off. In this way, working with particular passages, they demonstrate a creative way of engaging with the biblical text alongside ordinary folk and their ordinary circumstances.[3]

To this day, it remains a stimulating way of doing Bible study. When I devised my action-research project for the DMin on the Manor Estate in east Sheffield, I found myself engaging in participatory Bible study to improve the morale of a beleaguered congregation who had lost their church building and were at a low ebb, close to closure. In developing these Bible studies, *Mark at Work*, along with Walter Wink's *Transforming Bible Study* were very influential.[4] Through that process I discovered a creative and

---

2. For illustrations of what John means, see Vincent, *Hope from the City*, pts. 2–3.

3. Davies and Vincent, *Mark at Work*.

4. I discuss this way of developing Wink's approach in an article I wrote for *Education in Church Today* (Duffield, "Bible Study"). Robin Pagan's helpful step-by-step guide on how to move from consideration of one's context (see primacy 1) to the Bible and on toward practice (see primacy 5) is included in my article in *Bible and Practice* (Duffield, "From Bible to Ministry Projects").

participative way of doing Bible study that went beyond the rather personal and psychological perspective of Wink to a more socially orientated practice.

Bibliography

Davies, John D., and John J. Vincent. *Mark at Work*. Abingdon, UK: Bible Reading Fellowship, 1986.

Duffield, Ian K. "Bible Study for Personal and Social Transformation." *Education in Church Today* 6 (1992), 6–9.

———. "From Bible to Ministry Projects." In *Bible and Practice*, edited by Christopher Rowland and John J. Vincent, 67–68. British Liberation Theology 4. Sheffield: UTU, 2001.

Vincent, John J. *Christ in the City: The Dynamics of Christ in Urban Theological Practice*. Sheffield: UTU, 2013.

———. *Hope from the City*. London: Epworth, 2000.

Wink, Walter. *Transforming Bible Study*. Rev. ed. Eugene, OR: Wipf & Stock, 1980.

10

Meeting John Vincent: Context, Witness, and Radical Humility

Kevin Ellis

I FIRST MET JOHN Vincent when he preached at the ordination of a Methodist presbyter whom I trained with at the Queen's Foundation in Birmingham. I had known of John for over four decades. I had gone to the same school as one of his children, worshiped in a church near where he ministered, and my parents had regularly invited students connected with the UTU for meals. John has therefore had an influence over my development as a biblical scholar, minister, evangelist, and human being.

But until recently, as part of the latest PhD cohort to go through UTU, I had not engaged with John's work at any length nor spent any time in his presence seeing him at work. The context of my research, that of rural Wales, could not in some ways be more different than the urban places where John poured himself out as he sought to make sense of the gospel with those whom he walked alongside and who walked alongside him. John's welcome of me into the wider UTU family is typical of him. His primary concern as always is that theology should make sense in local context. For John, location can be as decisive as theology as an ingredient in the hermeneutical cycle.[1]

As a biblical scholar, John worked hard that his interpretation should be consonant with the contexts in which the text was written and in which they both have been and are now interpreted. This is an example par

---

1. Vincent, *Christ in the City*, 36.

excellence of scholarship being rooted in the life of local church communities.[2] Some of the practical ways he encouraged engagement with the text have been used by myself and by others.

This short piece sets out the reasons for why I am, and will be, profoundly grateful for his prophetic inspiration and the shadow he has cast as I have wrestled with how to do theology locally. I want to build my piece around the themes of contextual theology, witness, and radical humility.

Contextual Theology

John's ministry as an urban practitioner in Burngreave and Pitsmoor, as well as within the UTU, is rooted in context. His theology and biblical interpretations are authentic because the results are shaped by his experience of the city of Sheffield and by Sheffielders from different walks of life. John's emphasis on location or context as the starting point for all theology is something that is now shared by contextual and some practical theologians and is rooted in numerous versions of the pastoral or hermeneutical circle.

What I may say is distinctive and delightful about the approach fashioned at the UTU by John and others is that the voices of those the contextual theologian travels with are heard, reflected upon, and valued. Too often it is possible for voices to be heard without properly being included or heard only in part as the theologian seeks to shape their conclusions by what they think they have heard on the ground. This is a perennial problem of short-term academic projects and/or evangelistic initiatives of the church at local, regional, or national levels. John's commitment to being in a particular place and immersing himself in it over a lengthy period is countercultural, refreshing, and consonant with the God of justice whom he seeks to proclaim and serve. It allows the theologian to begin to see face-to-face rather than in part, although acknowledging that our understanding is always partial.

The contextual theologian may have a particular skill set and gifts to offer but is one among many in trying to discern what God may be saying. John was, and is, unafraid to learn from others. His Burngreave Ashram was a case in point, rooting following Jesus in a multifaith and multiracial setting and allowing it to shape, and be shaped, by radical scholarship and dispersed community living.[3] The same traits were present in the origins

2. Davies and Vincent, *Mark at Work*, 10–12.
3. See http://www.ashram.org.uk/.

of the UTU in Pitsmoor, which brought together a research center with a commitment to listening and the desire to create a place of hope without prescriptive ideas of what that hope might look like.[4]

In addition, I would have to say that his commitment to ensuring that the Scriptures, particularly the gospel narratives, are used in a way to shape a Christian and theological response to issues in community is exemplary, combining within his exegesis the commitment to trying to understand what the text means for the original hearers (insofar as that can be determined) and what it means for the communities he serves. His theology is so intertwined with Christian community because John is foremost someone who seeks to follow Christ with others. He writes: "It seemed to me, further, that the calling of a theologian always had to be secondary to the calling to be a disciple—or, more pertinently, that a theological vocation was impossible except as a development of a discipleship vocation."[5] Similarly, he writes in *Faithfulness in the City*: "Discipleship to Jesus lies as a determinative . . . [It] is more a basic assumption lying behind the practice, than a constant reference point. Yet, the assumption is decisive."[6] This has offered me a consistent challenge to wrestle with what it means for me to follow Jesus, which at times for the minister is a harder question than endeavoring to answer the question what it means for others to follow the way of the Messiah.

Witness

One of John's greatest gifts to those around him has been his articulation of what it means to be a follower of Jesus Christ in the twenty-first century. To describe John as an evangelist may raise a wry smile or two, but this is more because of how evangelists and evangelism are perceived than of how John embodies his faith. It seems to me his witness has been to keep the idea of Jesus the Radical at the forefront of his work, whether in ministry in the church and the academe, at the Ashram, or in the UTU. His participation in the UTU's Kingdom Evangelism Project is illustrative of his desire to ensure that what is shared with those within and outside the church about Jesus is consonant with radical scholarship.[7] John offered some of the bibli-

---

4. See Vincent, *Christ in the City*, 18–20.
5. Vincent, "Towards an Urban Theology," 4–17.
6. Vincent, *Faithfulness in the City*, 290.
7. See https://utusheffield.org.uk/kingdombasedevangelism/.

cal resources, especially around how to engage with the Gospels of Mark and John.[8] The conclusion reached in the material that disciples of Jesus are those who become "fellow-workers, co-healers, co-proclaimers" is consonant with the teaching John Vincent has offered over several decades.

In his ministry, the founder of UTU has endeavored to democratize theology. Although its PhD program has been enormously successful, as has its ability to gather scholars and leaders together, John's primary aim has been to enable good theology by "ordinary people" to happen in some of England's most marginal places. While many wondered whether the fruit of theologies of liberation nurtured in Latin American countries could be transplanted into a Western context, John and his colleagues showed that it could be done. John noted with characteristic self-depreciation, and I think some humor, that he was unaware that he was engaging in liberation theology until it was pointed out that this was the case.

I have often said that in UTU we were following a gospel-based methodology, based on a contextual Bible practice, and then discovered that others elsewhere were doing similarly and calling it liberation theology.[9] John immediately adds that people will talk about "liberation theology," whereas for twenty-five years he had talked about "gospel theology" and no one had noticed. There is an element of John's ministry that has been prophetic, and thus ignored. Those with power have usually been uncomfortable with the prophets, and prophets have had the skills to deal with such people and groups. John's bearing of consistent witness has no doubt been costly at a personal level at times; and for his willingness to pay such a price, church communities throughout the UK and beyond have a cause to be grateful.

Radical Humility

I suspect that this point will be the one which John is least comfortable with. John Vincent has poured his life into mission and ministry in my home city. With colleagues and friends, John has helped shaped theological thinking in urban areas. The preface to *Christ in the City*, with its list of former doctoral students and academic partners, reads like a veritable Who's Who of contextual theology and gospel studies.[10] John obviously more than holds his own in their company, as is further evidenced by his

---

8. Urban Theological Union, "Kingdom Evangelism."
9. Vincent, *Christ in the City*, 28.
10. Vincent, *Christ in the City*, 100.

contributions to the British New Testament Conference and to his work in partnership with several university Departments of Theology and Biblical Studies, most notably, perhaps, Sheffield. John could, if he had chosen, held positions of greater influence in the academe and the church. I suspect, and I am glad that this is the case, that he is more comfortable in places that are edgier, where truth telling in the manner of the prophets is easier.

John has also committed himself to learning and relearning. In areas of research, he has welcomed new methodologies if they enable contextual theology to ask deeper questions. This is seen in his embrace of ethnography, particularly the way it allows the voices of those whom we are working with to speak.[11] Andrew Bradstock and Christopher Rowland include John in their reader of *Radical Christian Writings*.[12] Vincent's "O.K., Let's Be Methodists" is positioned between Oscar Romero and the Kairos Document. This, I suspect, will be met with outright or diffident deflection. Nevertheless, the continuing existence of UTU and the engagement with urban theology more generally are testimony to John's work in this area, especially at times when his commitment to context as well as to Christ has not always been welcomed.

John has been, and remains, a gift to the church, scholarship, and community of Sheffield. As I said at the beginning of this piece, John had cast a shadow over my progress and development as a minister and scholar. Sometimes, when you meet your heroes, something of the sheen is removed. With John this is not the case; he has been consistently encouraging, enthusiastic, and challenging. This is the hallmark of the man and his ministry. This is the case because he has committed himself to working and walking with others, not all of whom have always agreed with him, and seeking always to allow the gospel to which he has devoted his life to have the last word. There is a tenacious humility to John that is radical. It is a gift to us at the UTU and has been a blessing to me.

The Rev. Dr. Kevin Ellis: Vicar of Bro Madryn in the Diocese of Bangor and UTU trustee, he already holds a PhD in the New Testament and is a PhD graduate of UTU

---

11. Vincent, *Christ in the City*, 34–36.
12. Vincent, "O.K., Let's Be Methodists."

Bibliography

Davies, John D., and John J. Vincent. *Mark at Work*. London: Bible Reading Fellowship, 1986.

Urban Theology Union. "Kingdom Evangelism." UTU Sheffield, Sept. 2021. https://utusheffield.org.uk/wp-content/uploads/2021/09/Kingdom-Evangelism-Pack-2021-Section-B.pdf.

Vincent, John J. *Christ in the City: The Dynamics of Christ in Urban Theological Practice*. Sheffield: UTU, 2013.

———. *Hope from the City*. London: Epworth, 2000.

———. "New Faith in the City." In *Faithfulness in the City*, edited by John J. Vincent, 290–306. New York: Monad, 2003.

———. "O.K., Let's Be Methodists." In *Radical Christian Writings: A Reader*, edited by Andrew Bradstock and Christopher Rowland, 280–84. Oxford: Blackwell, 1984.

———. "Towards an Urban Theology." *New Blackfriars* 64 (1983), 4–17.

11

John Vincent, Mark's Gospel, and the Fusion of Horizons

David McLoughlin

Two very different European thinkers visited the Jesuit Boston College in the 1970s: the Methodist theologian, Bible scholar, and community activist John Vincent and the recently retired German hermeneutical philosopher Hans Georg Gadamer. A superficial reading of their biographies and works might suggest they had little in common, but as a student of Gadamer's work since my teens and a longtime admirer and postgraduate student of John Vincent, I would like to suggest that the great philosopher gives us some key ideas that in fact clarify the project John has been engaged in since his own doctoral work in the 1960s with Oscar Cullmann and Karl Barth in Basel.

A Profound Obsession

John's doctoral research on discipleship in Mark began a lifetime's dialogue with the First Gospel, which has born, and continues to bear, extraordinary fruit. When I first joined a group of postgrads at UTU in 2008, John's engagement with Mark was good-naturedly seen by some as excessive to the point of obsession, suggesting that the other gospels were a falling away from the purity of Mark in much the way that Harnack saw the emergence of the post-Constantinian "Catholic Church" as the demise of the simplicity and purity of the primitive Jesus movement! In reality, John's project is something altogether much more profound, demanding, and ongoing.

Gadamer in his mature work *Truth and Method*, published in German the same year John defended his dissertation, locates the act of understanding, of coming to truth, as one that takes our finitude, our engagement, and involvement, and so the partiality and particularity of our experience, not as a barrier to understanding but precisely the conditions that make real understanding possible. We engage from the present concerns and interests of our lives, our "prejudices or prejudgments," in an "anticipation of completeness." A completeness that ultimately escapes us here and now but that is truly an anticipation "on the way" to something coherent, meaningful, and whole.[1] Gadamer's primary texts for dialogue were Plato's *Dialogues*, Aristotle's *Ethics*, Hegel, and Heidegger, and the poetry of Celan, Goethe, Hölderlin, and Rilke. Around these he reflected fruitfully and creatively throughout his long life. He died at 102 in Heidelberg in 2002.

A consequence of this for Gadamer was that our understanding involves us bringing the horizon of our previous understanding and judgments, including the influences of the traditions and communities we come from, into conversation with the prejudgments of the "other," either a person or a text. In the conversation that ensues, a fusion of horizons can take place, so that when we inevitably end the conversation, each of our perspectives will have been affected, our prejudgments challenged and perhaps modified and enriched; even though we still do not share exactly the same horizon of meaning. And all of this leads to greater and more informed practice and engagement since our outlooks have been inevitably stretched and informed by the encounter with the other.

John found the text that would engage him in conversation early in his working life. In Mark's Gospel he found the "other" whose horizon cannot be exhausted, and which has provided the challenge and stimulation to a deeply immersed life of scholarship, pastoral care, practical theology, and radical praxis.

Serendipity and Dialogue

The tradition of Methodism that John comes from resonates well with the hermeneutical approach of Gadamer of conversation, the sharing and merging of horizons, the willingness to come with presuppositions from

---

1. Gadamer, *Wahrheit und Methode*.

personal experience and knowledge, open to challenge and, if necessary, change. But to this John also brings quintessentially English elements of a sense of the serendipitous, a ready humor at once dry, wry, but gentle, and a profound humility and capacity to receive from the unexpected dialogue partner who walks in off the street or is encountered in the mundane. His normal context is not the halls of great universities but the streets of urban Britain.

A simple example. My research at UTU was on the changing role of the Bible in Christian activist movements. At one session I was giving a short paper to the wider PhD research seminar. It was on the method used in the 1950s and 60s in Young Christian Worker groups in Britain and France to think and live in the tension between critical issues in their working lives and the vision of the kingdom in Jesus's teaching and practice in the gospels. At the end of my paper there was a short silence, and then John burst out laughing and told us, rather ruefully, that later in the week he was giving a talk to Sheffield SCM (Student Christian Movement) students. The matter of his talk was, he had thought, contemporary and his own, but the substance of what he was saying was already in the praxis of those young workers fifty years previously! Unperturbed, he delighted in a new perspective on the emergence of practice-based contextual readings and told us he would now celebrate those young Christian workers in his own presentation.

This led into a fascinating discussion in the seminar, in part about loss and gain within Christian history, where often our role is to gather the fragments and rediscover the whole that has been lost. Gadamer would have seen this as part of the hermeneutical circle (really a spiral) where again and again we come back to foundations (with John to the Gospel of Mark) but each time with all the layered richness of the history of success and failure of our efforts in between.

In this process John is again revealed as the best of tutors. His careful reading and sparse annotation of student texts lead to suggestions that strengthen the students' own work. He has a good eye for the unnecessary and applies Ockham's razor with unfailing precision. The student immediately sees what needs to be left out, at this moment, for greater precision and a clearer argument. Yet he regularly recommends the excised material be kept as the basis for further development at a later time. Nothing is wasted. John has a gift for seeing and highlighting the particular, the unique, or personal comment that can be further developed to give a work that originality that another might have missed. And he can do this across the Christian traditions, always open to and encouraging of the particular voices from sacramental, evangelical, Pentecostal, and other traditions. This openness to the Word in its multiple forms reminds me of the poet Manley Hopkins lamenting in his sonnet "God's Grandeur" the worst excesses of the Industrial Revolution but still seeing how the divine can yet be encountered anywhere:

> For all this, nature is never spent;
> There lives the dearest freshness deep down things.[2]

This essential trusting hope that never leaves John has enabled him to build networks across the Atlantic, across Europe and the countries of the Global South.

UTU has been a deceptive entity. From the start it was a fine center for engaged pastoral ministerial training, with a small but good library and resource center. But through John's vision and the generous collaboration of his closest colleagues and supporters, it is so much more; it is an ecumenical matrix of radical discipleship. There, unlikely but creative encounters happen with its members and students, the neighborhood, and its international scholars and visitors, who keep returning, all providing unique aids to further creativity. I, like so many others, always come away from UTU feeling I have been listened to and heard, and knowing I have learned something from others that I would have struggled to find elsewhere. John Vincent's vision and spirit are at the heart of all of this. *Ad multos annos vivat!* May he continue to live, enlighten, and enliven us for many years to come.

David McLoughlin: Former Roman Catholic priest; Emeritus Fellow in Christian Theology, Newman University, Birmingham

Bibliography

Gadamer, Hans Georg. *Wahrheit und Methode: Grundzüge einer philosophischen Hermeneutik*. Tübingen: Mohr, 1960.

Manley Hopkins, Gerard. "God's Grandeur." Poetry Foundation, n.d. From *Gerard Manley Hopkins: Poems and Prose* (Penguin Classics, 1985). https://www.poetryfoundation.org/poems/44395/gods-grandeur.

2. Manley Hopkins, "God's Grandeur," lines 9–10.

12

Vincent's Radical Markan Project

James Bullock

I FIRST HEARD JOHN Vincent (and Grace) speak on a dark, rain-lashed November night at Church House in Rotherham in 2008. Having gone out of curiosity but with a strange sense of anticipation, I was immediately hooked in. The next day I searched for John's books online, and within a week a large airmail sack arrived from the US with a dozen or so books—someone in Washington State had also been a Vincent fan, for they were all from the same used bookstore. The following month I was at UTU discussing joining the MA Urban Theology course and a month or two later was regularly attending meetings at Burngreave Ashram. I started the MA in 2009 and spent endless hours in the cellar libraries of UTU. From this time, and for many years later, I was often in Sheffield every week for the course or another Ashram event or meeting. I graduated with the MA in 2012, winning the prizes for highest overall mark and the highest marked dissertation at York St. John University. I then embarked on research for a PhD, which because of COVID and personal issues, is still ongoing but, hopefully, soon drawing to a successful conclusion.

    What is it about John's work that so gripped me from that first meeting to today? I think, primarily, it is its immediacy and sense of urgency. John's interpretation of the Gospel of Mark is founded on an understanding of Mark as a narrative of urgency and commitment. For John, a few spare lines from Mark can be a source of rich understanding for the contemporary Christian disciple. Always there is the looping back and forth from ancient text to modern context that provides John's work with its life and mind-changing dynamic. Most of all, it is radical—in the best sense of the word—as well as uncompromising. John takes the bits he needs and sifts for what is significant. It is a method and a way of life that many more people should be aware of. Often deceptively simple and straightforward sentences contain worlds of meaning and are based on a lifetime's thinking.

It was *Secular Christ* (1968) that proved to be a source of theological thinking that drove my own research. Published the year I was born, it is still John's magnum opus, although he would (and I have heard him do it) disavow much of the content. Nevertheless, it is all in there. The mysteries of the kingdom, the significance of the parables, the dynamic of discipleship in its strangeness are all treated and explicated with astonishing radicality. My MA and PhD theses use John's interpretation of Mark and apply and contrast it with French philosophical theories of subjectivity and militant fidelity to a truth. But don't bother reading them. Read *Secular Christ*. It still stands.

Discerning Truth's Trajectory in Mark

In my PhD I aim to show that a Badiouian interpretation of Mark can shed new light on the radical subjectivity that I believe lies at the heart of that gospel. Badiou's own theory of truth (its emergence and transit through the world) and its connection to the subject are useful in that they provide a universal conceptual framework for the becoming of a subject and its relation to truth at any (or some) time in history. Badiou nominates Paul as the militant subject par excellence. Why? Because Paul (as opposed to Jesus himself) provides a model of how a militant, generic subject comes into being. The content of this subjectivization—resurrection—Badiou disavows as "a mythological assertion."[1] It is as a formal theoretical statement that "Christ is resurrected" fulfils the conditions of a founding event nominated by Paul—"detached from every objectivist assignation to the particular laws of a world or society yet concretely destined to become inscribed within a world and within a society."[2] Paul breaks with Jewish theology and history and announces a new truth to the world. The key conditions of the truth-bearing event—"a sort of grace supernumerary to every particularity"—are met under the name of Christ.[3] A name that supports only itself without

---

1. Badiou, *Saint Paul*, 107.
2. Badiou, *Saint Paul*, 107–8.
3. Badiou, *Saint Paul*, 109.

reference to knowledge as such. The name is addressed to all—without exception, Paul tells us—it is a generic production, a sui generis claim of equality. For Badiou, "The production of equality and the casting off, of thought, of differences are the material signs of the universal."[4]

Without, at this point, exploring in detail Badiou's theory of Paul, it is important to note that I see the conditions of universality and equality being met under the name "kingdom of God" in Mark. Also, that the model of fidelity to this truth—the model of militant subjectivity that Badiou identifies in the person or thought of Saint Paul—is better exemplified by the strange story of discipleship in Mark. The parabolic messages of Jesus concerning the realm of God in Mark 1–8 particularly seem to me to indicate both the universal, egalitarian nature of that realm and also, via Mark's narrative, how the process of subjectivization actually works. I assert that Mark 1–8 provides within it a much better model of truth and the subject than Paul, in both Badiouian terms and, as template for radical discipleship, sheds light on some of the shortcomings, both practical and theoretical, of Badiou's theory of truth and the subject.

Through the analysis of some aspects of Mark 1–8, I refer to John Vincent's contemporary view of radical discipleship based on Mark. John has naturally been chosen because of his exploration in theory and advocacy in practice of radical discipleship based on an interpretation of Mark.

Vincentian Mark

John's radical Markan project—theory and practice—was announced to the world half a century ago with the publication of *Secular Christ* (1968) in both the UK and US. Prior to that there had been *Christ and Methodism* (1965) and *Here I Stand: The Faith of a Radical* (1967). The first a plea for a new radical Christology to revive the Methodist Church; the second a barnstorming assault on the complacency of the wider church in the face of decline and disinterest in postwar secular Britain and, specifically, the new idealisms of the sixties, where bomb-damaged Victorian England and its churches were being swept away both culturally and literally in Harold Wilson's new technological age.

Significantly, despite being couched somewhat in the language of sixties theological radicalism—e.g., the "new Reformation" of J. A. T. Robinson's *Honest to God* (1964)—both books were "radical" in the sense of

---

4. Badiou, *Saint Paul*, 109.

advocating a return to the roots of Methodism and of Christianity rather than throwing out the bits that the secular sixties had decided were no longer relevant.[5]

Neither conservative-evangelical nor liberal-radical, John in *Secular Christ* proclaims a "Christocentric Radicalism."[6] Coming through and out of the Methodist Sacramental Fellowship, Donald Soper's Order of Christian Witness, the Methodist Peace Fellowship, the founding of the Campaign for Nuclear Disarmament (CND), and the Labour movement, John could see the necessary corrective that those radical directions provided to the Methodist movement in particular and also to the wider church but, at the same time, saw that to keep close to Jesus's side demanded a different, less programmatic approach. A new way of being the church of Jesus in the modern world, taking Wesley at his word (and deed): universal, open to all, small, light on its feet, being church wherever it's needed or wherever it's least wanted. Most of all, being—in its situation and existence—of and alongside the poor and excluded. More was to come, in John's systematization of these views: *Secular Christ* (1968).

In *Secular Christ* the core of his radical Markan Christology can be found. As John states, "I was so grasped by the mystery, singularity, and mutual consistency of some of the things which Mark (above all) had to say—and the significance of some of the things he did not say—that I wished to expose others to the freshness and theological depth of the gospels' hints at solving the insolvable."[7] What he was later to refer to as "radical Jesus" was based from the outset on a particular view of the Mark's Gospel (Mark 1–8 in particular) and the Jesus who can be found within this small text. It would not be an exaggeration to say that John's whole view of

---

5. Later there would be many other publications: The UTU series New City Specials, a trilogy for the Methodist Church in 1989 published during John's year as president of the Methodist Conference, which identified and addressed the issues facing church and society in the following decade, the 1990s; and the British Liberation Theology series edited by Chris Rowland and John. There were some books around a specific topic: *Christ in a Nuclear World* (1962), *The Race Race* (1970), *Alternative Church* (1976), or *O.K., Let's Be Methodists* (1984), an updated analysis of the state of Methodism in the UK. As well as a trilogy that spans three decades telling the story of the Urban Theology Unit (the "university of the streets" founded by John in inner-city Sheffield in 1970) and the Ashram Community—another inner-city project based on community living and alternative church and worship models: *Into the City* (1982), *Hope from the City* (2000) and *Christ in the City* (2013).

6. Vincent, *Secular Christ*, 16.

7. Vincent, *Secular Christ*, 11.

Jesus, the church, and the role of the church—whatever that might look like—in society is founded almost entirely on Mark 1–8. This viewpoint has led to a lifetime's ministry in the city, many publications, a theological university of the streets—the Urban Theology Unit (now Union)—and a church/community/monastery spread over many lives and buildings in the poorest parts of Sheffield—the Ashram Community. Why? What is the radical dynamic in Mark that founds such a project?

It seems to me, there are three significant moves that John takes in *Secular Christ*. One, his Christology does not "throw out" the mysteries of Jesus but actually embraces them; two, he situates this mysterious Markan Jesus in the secular world; three, he makes the two things together a question of subjectivity: "What form of human existence is demanded by the whole Jesus-phenomenon which creates the New Testament? What does this Jesus-story say about man in his nonreligious existence?"[8] For John, what is at issue is partly what the word "secular"—a phrase very much au courant in sixties theology—means.[9] This is not about "secularizing" Jesus or "demythologizing." Rather, it is about seeing Jesus in his essential secularity. John's understanding of secularity follows Bonhoeffer: for John, the conception of God in the modern age was not all about history but "determined by Bonhoeffer's picture of Christ—a picture which was of what I would call a 'Secular Christ.'"[10] For John, the idea of secularity is not about "fitting" the Christ of the gospels into a modern philosophical category or, indeed, making claims about a "new age" of humankind for which a "new" Christianity is required. For John (as for Wesley) everything needed is already there in the gospel, and not only that, but the Christ of the gospel is, in fact, the one fit for the "modern age" because he comes before "the perversions of religion, of philosophy, of ecclesiology. The Christ who has been perverted by these things is not the Christ of the New Testament. The Christ of the New Testament is discovered in his essential secularity."[11]

Neither is it about being "saved": "The Christ-events, delivered from their straitjacket within the salvation-scheme, become life-giving for the

---

8. Vincent, *Secular Christ*, 29.

9. In this John is influenced by Harvey Cox's *Secular City* (1965), and especially by Carl Michalson's *Worldly Theology* (1967). John worked alongside Michalson at Drew University, NY, in 1964.

10. Vincent, *Secular Christ*, 47.

11. Vincent, *Secular Christ*, 51.

Christian. Must not theology now follow experience?"[12] So, John works outward from the Jesus event to the world, in fact insists that this process of outworking takes place within each secular situation. John's deployment of the concept of outworking in terms of gospel interpretation and discipleship practice plays a key role in my critique of the French philosopher Alain Badiou's idea of the faithful subject in my PhD at UTU. Not least because the notion of working out—of "outworking"—within the world the possibilities or consequences of an idea or understanding of a text or historical event is central to and mirrored by Badiou's own theory of event, truth and subjectivization.

But now, I discuss John's broader understanding of radical discipleship from *Secular Christ* and its later development in *Radical Jesus*.

The Strangeness of Jesus

John emphasizes the particularity of the gospel, the peculiar situated-ness of Jesus in first-century Palestine. As John points out, it is precisely these "accidentals" that make the Jesus story so strange.[13] Furthermore, this seemingly arbitrary site fuels an even stranger tale of clashes with authority and a highly unusual collection of characters. Why these people? Why this particular action? John's explanation is that another reason for this "strangeness" is that the theology and mission of Jesus are "unashamedly discriminatory."[14] This represents part of his method of ignoring all the common categories of power and social relations current in first-century Palestine. Jesus acts as though they don't exist. In this sense John is right when he says that Christ's common humanity is a theological commonplace.[15] What is important is not that in some respects he was a man like other men—emphasizing "the life" or the secularity of Jesus in that sense doesn't take us very far—it is precisely in the "strangeness" that we find the "meaning" of Jesus:

> It is not the points at which Jesus was like us, but the points at which he was unlike us that are instructive. Not the points at which "miracle" intervenes, necessarily, but the points at which he or any man handles what we all do but handles it differently,

12. Vincent, *Secular Christ*, 32.
13. Vincent, *Secular Christ*, 70.
14. Vincent, *Secular Christ*, 70.
15. Vincent, *Secular Christ*, 69.

handles it significantly, handles it in a sense finally—these are the points at which man betrays genius, lordship, or, one would guess, divinity.[16]

So, Jesus does things differently, oddly, and without regard for convention. Strange indeed.

Mark's Gospel: A Secular Jesus

John views Mark "as a reliable witness to the earliest forms of the stories of Jesus" and as a "conceptual" narrative designed to be meaningful—not a biography as such.[17] Mark wrote for those who had not known Jesus. The Markan Gospel is a constructed narrative about what Jesus, during his short ministry, did (even the talking is doing). But being concerned with the things of the world does not preclude something "other" than those things. Mark is a secular gospel in the sense that the elements that make up the narrative are things and people situated in first-century Palestine, but there is an element of something else that "indicates 'something new'" in the history of man and God.[18]

Jesus: A Christology of Action

John puts aside debates, current at the time, about the names or titles of Jesus: "It is not a question of titles but of actions of Jesus, which he then justifies and explains by words."[19] In fact, the mystery of who Jesus was and what the exact nature of his mission on earth was are no more likely to be "discovered" in 1968, now, or in the future. His own disciples and family did not "recognize" him. Whether Jesus was Son of Man, Son of God, or Messiah is, for John, irrelevant: "He is what he is, and he does what he does."[20] Indeed, John believes, Jesus himself tells us that he we cannot discover him by bringing any preconceptions with us—he is a "stumbling block" to our understanding. This caesura or impasse that is built into the gospel narrative is deliberate and important. If we "knew" who Jesus was

---

16. Vincent, *Secular Christ*, 70.
17. Vincent, *Secular Christ*, 74.
18. Vincent, *Secular Christ*, 79.
19. Vincent, *Secular Christ*, 84.
20. Vincent, *Secular Christ*, 86.

and the exact nature of his purpose, we would simply need to follow his program—there would be no need to work out again and again in every generation what we should do now to follow him. This conceptual gesture blocks our understanding as it did that of the disciples—we don't know, because to "know" means to allow "Jesus" to become part of the encyclopedia of knowledge, part of what already is, and therefore something old and no longer new. It also prevents truth becoming absolutism. Whatever "truth" is contained within the Markan record, it is always contingent. It's "up for grabs" at every moment. Truth—the kingdom of God—is always seen in hints, never in full reality, because what it means has to be "worked out" in the world. What Jesus may or may not be called or what his meaning may be is "because Christology hangs upon the action of Jesus and the action of the questioner."[21] The stumbling block is that "the deeds of Jesus are really not what we came looking for, either as an assessment of human existence at its best or as a manifestation of a powerful God. But that is all there is for us to find."[22] So, the meaning of Jesus, demonstrated in Mark in particular, is significant action. For John, Jesus is demonstrating his unique connection with the divine or with God: "Jesus is the secular activity of the hidden God."[23] In my interpretation of Badiou, Jesus is the model of the militant subject demonstrating his fidelity to truth.

The Meaning of the Kingdom in Mark

For John, as we would expect, the meaning of the kingdom in Mark lies in what Jesus does. Jesus announces the nearness of a "kingdom" at the beginning of Mark's narrative and gathers followers around him. The coming of the kingdom and Jesus with it is accompanied by powers of healing. John deals with the "miraculous" nature of Jesus's healing as follows: "It is quite sufficient for men to see the deeds and by faith to become involved in them either as recipients (in the case of healing) or as participants (in the case of discipleship)."[24] The miracles are hints of the kingdom in their newness as well as an indication of kingdom practice. Further indications of the meaning of the kingdom follow: Jesus has meals with publicans and sinners (Mark 2:14)—people outside the law, degraded and accursed. It is

---

21. Vincent, *Secular Christ*, 87.
22. Vincent, *Secular Christ*, 88.
23. Vincent, *Secular Christ*, 89.
24. Vincent, *Secular Christ*, 98.

a sign that the kingdom of heaven has been opened by Jesus, cause not only for celebration for all but as a performative act to show what the new kingdom looks like. In those instances or moments, "the kingdom becomes dynamically present . . . in the deeds of Jesus."[25] Jesus is acting as though he is God and the kingdom of God itself is his kingdom. He brings a new power (*exousia*) in the form of his words and deeds together. He is both acting out and providing a commentary on his actions at the same time, obliquely—to explain literally would mean objectifying the kingdom, and the kingdom will come about only through the actions of those subject to its truth.

In Mark, "the kingdom is hidden within the world."[26] There is no separation between the kingdom and the world. Like Badiou's empty set, it is part and parcel of the world's makeup: "The kingdom is genuinely within the secular, part of it, met within it."[27] The task of the disciple, therefore, in order to meet with the kingdom, is to do as Jesus did, to act in a way that embodies the kingdom, but not, however, to do exactly what Jesus did. The acts of Jesus exemplify ways of acting as though the kingdom is near. So, we make our response "to the hidden kingdom 'by faith'—that is, without seeing whether the ultimate, final, or transcendental in fact are involved."[28] The faithful subject or disciple is not, therefore, given any answers to what truth or the kingdom may or may not be. Nor is she given any guarantees of personal fulfilment, "eternal life," "salvation," or any other kind of positivist response, secular or otherwise. As John emphasizes, "The issues of the kingdom . . . can only be dealt with indirectly."[29] They can only be dealt with at all by helping the man by the roadside, breaking bread with outcasts, "healing" the sick or insane, etc. That, or something like it in your part of the woods, is what is on offer in terms of finding the kingdom of God or its "secrets."

So, Christ is not secular because, from the sixties viewpoint, we live in a "secular" age and "modern man" (in the terminology of the time) needs a Jesus to match the times. For John, the Jesus of Mark is secular *already*: "Jesus strictly represents the secularization of God," and the good news he

---

25. Vincent, *Secular Christ*, 101.
26. Vincent, *Secular Christ*, 118.
27. Vincent, *Secular Christ*, 119.
28. Vincent, *Secular Christ*, 119.
29. Vincent, *Secular Christ*, 120.

announces is that "the ultimately acceptable lies hidden within the deeds of the world."[30]

Discipleship: The Faith That Works

John develops his theory of discipleship in *Secular Christ* by outlining some of the preconditions that exist in the becoming of a disciple. First, a disciple's response is always in and about action; specifically about participation in the deeds of Jesus—"through concrete obedience to Jesus, through responding to the hidden presence of the Jesus-issue, the kingdom, in ordinary everyday decisions."[31] Second, the disciple has a change of mind or of heart or of thinking (*metanoia*). This means "believing in the new fact of the kingdom represented by Jesus."[32] Here, in Badiouian terms, the kingdom is the truth carried by the event that is Jesus. Third, faith is everything. But what is it? It is not unexpected to find that for John faith is about being involved in God's action in the world: "the preparedness to act on the unprovable" and, what is more, "to operate as if the unprovable—the presence of God within Jesus of Nazareth, the presence of the ultimate within the secular—were demonstrable."[33]

These then are the preconditions for the faithful subject or disciple. In talking about the characteristics of discipleship presented in the gospels, John talks about discipleship as "Jesus-related existence."[34] It's about being with Jesus in his deeds; and so being with Jesus in his actions in order to meet the needs of others, not the self. This is not about choice but a participation in a "way" or a procedure, we might say, not an aspect of personality.[35] Such participation can mean "suffering and deprivation at the hands of the world."[36] These are the consequences, not to say the prerequisites, of discipleship.

---

30. Vincent, *Secular Christ*, 124.
31. Vincent, *Secular Christ*, 127.
32. Vincent, *Secular Christ*, 129.
33. Vincent, *Secular Christ*, 132.
34. Vincent, *Secular Christ*, 137.
35. Vincent, *Secular Christ*, 138.
36. Vincent, *Secular Christ*, 139.

The "Outworkings" Method and the Dynamics of Christ

John's more recent explanation of the Markan Jesus and of discipleship appears in *Radical Jesus* (2004). However, alongside his work on Jesus, John has also continued to develop his radical method of biblical interpretation in *Outworkings: Gospel Practice and Interpretation* (2005).

This method of practice and interpretation is based on an understanding of the New Testament as not a once-in-history story of God's action through Jesus but "the first staging, the first performance, the opening night; of a pattern of God-directed praxis that is to be continued, repeated, acted again and again in the history of the world."[37] Gospel practice criticism, therefore, aims to establish a biblical critical method that might provide signposts to a gospel practice—developing a project based on Jesus's original performative project in the New Testament: "If the Bible describes the 'Acts of God' or 'God's Project(s),' then our interest should be with consequent 'acts' and 'projects,' which continue or reflect or are based upon the primary divine acts and projects."[38] So, practice criticism is a bridge between event and effect, past and present. For John, the gospel stories and their "history in-practice" function "as an interpretative and provocative medium between action and action, between practice and practice."[39] The stories are told to demonstrate and communicate that whatever happening took place was significant. Others in history have acted based on their interpretation of the significance of the event clothed by story. But how does the would-be disciple now act "truthfully" or "with fidelity" (to use Badiouian terms) to the significance of the story—how can the disciple "get to" the kernel of truth of the event that created the story? For John, as for Badiou, the original "truth" remains obscure; its significance for the reader now is opened up only within an exploration of what the originating action/event/happening might look like if something happened today that might open up or contain within it something of what prompted the original act. The truth or meaning of the act itself can only, if ever, be discerned infinitely, i.e., any understanding is eternally post facto. After the original event; after the new event, all understanding is post practice. Meaning, as such, is postponed.

---

37. Vincent, *Outworkings*, 3.
38. Vincent, *Outworkings*, 4.
39. Vincent, *Outworkings*, 5.

So, John, while maintaining an anti-ideological, anti-philosophical stance by placing all interpretation in the sphere of praxis, does, nevertheless, by the formal act of developing a method of practice open up the possibility that the method communicates to us as much about the theory set out in *Secular Christ* and *Radical Jesus*, as it is does about a "blind" or pure praxis in itself, which John occasionally treats as being the sole point and end point of all theology.

The core of this method of "Practice-Response"[40] or, perhaps, New Testament criticism in the context of developing faithful practice evolves around the question: How does a subject, a disciple, a group of disciples, judge the fidelity of their practice in comparison to the truth of the originating event? Here the judgment of the significance of the practice and, hence, of the meaning of the text that inspired it is made "not in terms of ideas, conclusions, literary comparisons or analyses" but rather in terms of its outcomes or, as John names it, "outworkings."[41]

For John, a practice-oriented criticism focuses on the response to the story rather than the interpretation: "So that the hearer will go and do something which is predicated by it, or provoked by it, or coherent with it. The primary action in the story has produced another action."[42]

What, then, is the method? Essentially, the method is not in the interpretative practice but in the person and the place or subject and situation. John firmly places the practice of the disciple (or, in Badiou's terms, the faithful or militant subject) at the heart of practice criticism. Yes, he seems to say, people are people everywhere and everyone has the right to have a say, but the people who work out the significance of the gospel in the world are the people who have already been convoked by that gospel for that very purpose. It is the work of the disciple, primarily. First, the activity of the disciple is itself a *site* of "practice-response," "in which the text actually achieves some kind of present life."[43] In other words, the process is an entirely secular or practical one—it is not a literary enterprise.

Second, the *site* is also the *site as situation*. Where you are matters. Merely to understand the bias of the reader is one thing, but to hear or read

---

40. Vincent, *Outworkings*, 6.

41. Vincent, *Outworkings*, 6. The term "outworkings" is derived from the *Wirkungsgeschichte* method of Ulrich Luz, as developed in his three-volume commentary on Matthew (Luz, *Matthew*) and the introduction to his method in *Matthew in History*.

42. Vincent, *Outworkings*, 10.

43. Vincent, *Outworkings*, 10.

the word in the context of affluence is also to compound the offence. Hence, John offers the city, in particular, the poor city as the disciple situation to read, interpret, and act. The rich, the suburban dweller, the educated are still a tiny minority of the world's people—a specifically urban theological practice situated in the city may begin to mitigate this bias.[44]

The method writ large (of which the outworkings process is the underlying dynamic) is based on situation analysis, e.g., understand where you are, identify the need, find which bit of the gospel may help you develop a response and intentional practice. Use the material intentionally, share your story of how it worked. An urban practitioner "appropriates the Gospel stories as if they were descriptive of practice which is in fact their own."[45]

Christ in the City—the Dynamics of Christ in Urban Theological Practice

In *Christ in the City* (2013), John sets out his most recent and most comprehensive statement of the radical discipleship process, including his development of the practice criticism approach discussed above. He sets out models for each stage of the process. Although he explores different contexts, e.g., discipleship and ministry, community and politics, I will focus on the core procedure, which John calls "the dynamics of Christ." His procedure is a praxis-oriented hermeneutical process. The original meaning of Mark is closed off from us. We can seek out only elements within the text that we identify with and develop "a model of a series of 'immediate identifications' of elements in a Gospel Encounter, which lead on to a 'wider practice' of Elements of Jesus/God's project."[46]

The key stages of John's "dynamics of Christ" theologizing procedure are first to create an alternative analysis of the gospel situation and the contemporary situation via gospel situation analysis and gospel practice analysis—bringing together elements of the gospel with bits of our own world. This, John makes clear, is "a theology of process."[47] Next, the Jesus praxis cycle models how what Jesus does imparts to us the meaning of why he does it. And how by moving from one act to another, a new way of being

---

44. Vincent, *Christ in the City*, 11.
45. Vincent, *Outworkings*, 21.
46. Vincent, *Christ in the City*, 53.
47. Vincent, *Christ in the City*, 53.

is demonstrated. This is then delineated in the Jesus vocational cycle and the discipleship vocational cycle. Thus, "out of all this, new community and politics are created, and new understanding or 'truth' emerges—out of all this, 'theology' is born or reborn."[48] Truth (or new elements of a new world) is not constructed as such; it comes into being or emerges. It is, in a sense, carried into the world via the praxis of the radical disciple or subject.

John's key analogy of the actual process of discernment is, appropriately, a Sheffield one—the steel crucible. All the "bits" extracted or retained from the procedure described above are thrown together: "The situation characteristics and the gospel characteristics are both subjected to this kind of questioning in turn, to begin to get the feel of contrary elements and possible identifications. Then we bring bits of the gospel and bits of the situation into critical dialogue in order to push them together into a 'crucible.'"[49] Only some bits "spark" off other bits. John retains contingency throughout the model. This is not ideology. Finally, via the project, something new, which carries an element of the chemical composition of the originating Jesus praxis-event, *becomes*: "The dynamic, conflictual factors lead to something new—which combines elements of Situation and Gospel."[50] This becomes an embodiment of the new reality.

For John, "faith" in the New Testament is the preparedness to act in discipleship, community, and politics as if the utterly unprovable—that God accepts what belongs to Christ—were true. It is to "act boldly" as if the hidden were already plain. This symbol, this gift, is "both discriminatory, restricting itself to the deeds which are found to belong to Christ, and also indiscriminate, because all people and all history stand equally before the opportunity of acceptance and entry."[51] Like Badiou, John insists on both the indiscernibility (the hidden) and the unknowability (the unprovable) of truth. It is the fidelity (faith) of the disciple, the faithful subject, that is the signpost of truth.

So, John moves from the Gospel of Mark to radical discipleship and along the way establishes a new form of gospel criticism as he facilitates a procedure or method that faithful disciples can use to embody the gospel in ordinary, secular reality—now.

---

48. Vincent, *Christ in the City*, 62.
49. Vincent, *Christ in the City*, 66.
50. Vincent, *Christ in the City*, 67.
51. Vincent, *Secular Christ*, 167.

James Bullock: Primary school headteacher in Doncaster; MA graduate; and current researcher investigating the "faithful subject" in Alain Badiou, John Vincent, and the Gospel of Mark

Bibliography

Badiou, Alain. *Saint Paul: The Foundation of Universalism.* Translated by Ray Brassier. Cultural Memory in the Present. Stanford, CA: Stanford University Press, 2003.

Luz, Ulrich. *Matthew.* 3 vols. Edited by Helmut Koester. Translated by James E. Crouch. Minneapolis: Fortress, 2001–7.

———. *Matthew in History: Interpretation, Influence, and Effects.* Minneapolis: Fortress, 1994.

Robinson, John A. T. *Honest to God.* London, SCM, 1964.

Vincent, John J. *Alternative Church.* Belfast: Christian Journals, 1976.

———. *Christ and Methodism: Towards a New Christianity for a New Age.* London: Epworth, 1965.

———. *Christ in a Nuclear World.* Manchester: Crux, 1962.

———. *Christ in the City: The Dynamics of Christ in Urban Theological Practice.* Sheffield: UTU, 2013.

———. *Here I Stand: The Faith of a Radical.* London: Epworth, 1967.

———. *O.K., Let's Be Methodists.* London: Epworth, 1984.

———. *Outworkings: Gospel Practice and Interpretation.* Sheffield: UTU, 2005.

———. *The Race Race.* London: SCM, 1970.

———. *Radical Jesus: The Heart of Radical Discipleship.* Sheffield: Ashram, 2004.

———. *Secular Christ: A Contemporary Interpretation of Jesus.* London: Lutterworth, 1968.

PART V

The Primacy of Practice

Introduction

Orientation to the Primacy of Practice

IAN K. DUFFIELD

JOHN FREQUENTLY TALKS ABOUT "acted parables" and of "gospel projects" or "theological practice." All this reveals his antinomy to theory. Practice is primary, which is more a feature of Mark than other gospels, as it contains no parables or teaching discourses and is less obviously theological. Indeed, for John, practice comes before theory or even before doing theology. He sometimes talks of getting into things that then need a theology to understand them or defend them. Practice comes first.

John's lack of interest in theory, per se, and his pronouncements on practice must not be misunderstood. This is not activism for activism's sake, for the only practice he's interested in is gospel practice, and the only projects are gospel projects. In other words, John is always looking for an incarnation of the gospel, its enfleshment in secular life, its embodiment in particular practices. And the practices he encourages, therefore, are those that arise out of the gospel or more particularly that arise out of the dynamic between each particular situation and the gospel. In this way it is fundamentally dialogical or a way of doing what Tillich calls correlation (see below). And it's from this perspective, of course, that he identifies and promotes "practice interpretation" of Scripture. This is also why he labels gospel practice as an "outworking," i.e., the way the gospel, particularly Mark's Gospel, has a contemporary working out in our day (see, for example, Don Rudalevige's chapter). Thus it is that John doesn't dwell on the text as an artifact of the past, as a historical datum, but as a prelude to, or antecedent of, or archetype for, or a haunting provocation toward present practice. In a way, his articulation of outworkings is simply a logical extension of placing Mark's Gospel and current practice stimulated by that gospel at the forefront of his own reflection and activity. This is not an anti-intellectual stance but a demand that human intellect and biblical seriousness be at the service of contemporary embodiments of what is found in the text such that the past is reanimated, as it were, in a different form in the present.

So, John links Scripture with practice, hence the volume he edited with Chris Rowland,[1] and advocates "practice interpretation," i.e., allowing practice to influence the way Scripture is understood and interpreted. Others may go to other parts of Scripture, but John is endlessly satisfied (if that's the right word) with Mark; it is like Elijah's cruse of oil, it never runs out (1 Kgs 17). Similarly, there is always something to be done, some project to engage in, some program to instantiate. John is a doer, and a proactive doer at that. As they say, John doesn't like to let the grass grow under his feet, because his entrepreneurial instincts won't let him. As I once heard his elderly mother say to him: "What are you planning now, Johnny?" John, like some others in his family, is an entrepreneur, with a never-ending eye for an opportunity or opening or possibility—for what Frank Thewlis taught him was "the main chance." Not for John a getting lost in theory or wittering over details, because there's always something to be done. Practice is primary. And from the practice comes thought, which leads to new practice until the kingdom come.

Of course, such practice should have the "marks of the gospel" about it. It's not activity for the sake of activity. It is activity for the sake of the gospel. It is activity demanded of the disciple of Christ. And often, such practice takes a radical form. Hence, John as the radical disciple of this book's title: always looking for alternatives, always journeying on in faith and hope. Though John disdained his fellow Methodist Norman Vincent Peale's advocacy of the "power of positive thinking,"[2] in many ways John is a living testimony to its truth. John often says, don't focus on the negative, find something positive to have a go at. He knows how debilitating it can be to be looking backward (e.g., Lot's wife), so he wishes to look forward; even if doors are closed, you knock on another one (keep knocking); if you can't jump on one cart, jump on another; if one project fails, invent another, and try that and see what happens.

1. Rowland and Vincent, *Bible and Practice*.
2. Peale, *Power of Positive Thinking*.

Introduction to Part V

John talks about "Christology by imitation," i.e., he is more interested in what people do in imitating Christ in our day than being knowledgeable theologically or being able to rehearse christological debate. This is another aspect, if you will, of the primacy of practice and relates to the way John has introduced gospel practice criticism to the academy. There are various forms of biblical criticism, but again, John, although he knows them all, is not interested in being able to rehearse the arguments or to discuss their validity as a theoretical exercise. Rather, he is interested in understanding the biblical text in the light of practice. Applied theology talked about understanding the theology and then applying it; this classic approach was what I learned when I did the BD at King's College London. So, it was a relief to find John, having discovered that applying the theology I'd learned didn't go so well in practice—in fact, I'm not sure, now, whether it can be done. Having studied Paul Tillich for my MTh at King's, I was more interested in correlation: How do we find gospel answers to the realities we experience? And John appeared to me to offer a way into that that moved beyond personal/psychological/existential questions to correlating the gospel with social/communal/existential issues that were pressing.

John is not interested in applied theology or even practical theology, which tends to end up being more interested in theory or philosophy, but is much more interested in what he calls *outworkings*, the way the biblical text has gained another life or moved into a contemporary embodiment. In this way, John builds on a contemporary academic interest in the theology of interpretation of the text (especially by Ulrich Luz). But, yet again, John is interested, above all, in practice, so he extends this new form of criticism beyond what scholars would normally contemplate. John wants to know how the text has gained form, been enfleshed or incarnated, in the present day: Which texts have inspired which practice? How has this or that text been provocative for practice in which situations of life? Again, the academy is interested in the *Sitz im Leben* (the situation in life) of the early gospel writers and has become interested, in the history of interpretation, in understanding the *Sitz im Leben* of commentators down the centuries (like Luther); but John takes a radical step in his concern for the *Sitz im Leben* of contemporary gospel practitioners. Which situations lead us to which texts? Which texts lead to which contemporary practice? Again, with his concern for the urban, he wants to investigate what this means for urban discipleship: How is Christ evoked or imitated or enfleshed in the city today; how does incarnation happen now?

John, of course, has spent a lot of time imagining and investigating how aspects of the gospel may take form in our urban world and has spent even more time in experimenting in practice. The first volume of John's trilogy, *Into the City*, is in fact structured around key elements of the Jesus narrative and what that might look like today. So, the various chapters consider incarnation, healings, parables, acted parables, disciple groups, crucifixion, resurrection. And John has often used this format with groups at UTU as a way of looking creatively at Mark's Gospel to engender new responses, fresh outworkings.

Along with Professor John Rogerson of the Biblical Studies Department in Sheffield University, the Institute for Socio-Biblical Studies ran as a UTU summer school for many years. This engagement with practice interpretation led to the production of a number of volumes published by Deo/Brill, in a series edited by John, with two volumes edited by John Rogerson. This is explained on the back cover of issues thus: "Practice Interpretation takes the everyday social conditions of people as they are described in the Bible and looks at emerging issues that confront today's interpreters in daily life."[3] Of course, for John, "today's interpreters" need to be active practitioners prepared to engage not primarily with theory or with discussing issues, but with what their practice tells them. How is it, or how can it become, an outworking of the gospel, or a form of contemporary discipleship within a particular setting?

Bibliography

Peale, Norman Vincent. *The Power of Positive Thinking for Young People*. New York: Prentice-Hall, 1954.
Rogerson, John W., and John Vincent. *The Servant of God in Practice*. Practice Interpretation 6. Blandford Forum, UK: Deo, 2017.
Rowland, Christopher, and John J. Vincent, eds. *Bible and Practice*. Sheffield: UTU, 2001.
Vincent, John J. *Into the City*. London: Epworth, 1982.

---

3. See, e.g., back cover of Rogerson and Vincent, *Servant of God*.

13

Living Mark's Gospel in New England: Urban Ministry Projects

Don Rudalevige

IN 1993, A NETWORK of urban clergy from the northeastern United States went to a variety of urban sites in Britain, the most significant of which we thought was to be Belfast Central Mission, which had been recently bombed—by mistake; the IRA was aiming for the hotel next door. However, while in Belfast, we were urged to go to Sheffield, where John Vincent was doing amazing things in urban ministry. We changed our plans, hired a van, and made our way to Sheffield. In retrospect, after our time in Sheffield, we realized how John's vision was being implemented in Belfast by a group of courageous Methodists.

As a result of those few days in Sheffield, working under John's tutelage, the three of us who were from New England vowed to get the funds to create an urban ministry project, working closely with the UTU. I was to lead the US work, as I was the program director for the conference and had the most knowledge of Britain, having read theology at Mansfield College, Oxford.

In 1995, we got underway, working closely with John, who came over to the Boston area to meet nine site teams and pastors. It was to be a two-year endeavor, with the first year being devoted to biblical study—Mark, of course!—demographic research, neighborhood walks, and marshaling resources. We used texts and materials supplied by John, with whom we kept in close touch. The nine churches were divided into three cells, which met quarterly, with a tutor for each. At the end of the first year, each church site team was to have developed insights as to how to move forward missionally in their community. The idea was that at the end of that first year, the pastors, tutors, and I would go to Sheffield for ten days to develop a project that could be implemented in the coming year.

Why UTU?

But why come to the UTU? Why not stay in the US? We got asked this a lot! The answer is that the UTU under John's direction exuded a love for the city based in a Christian context, founded on responsible scriptural study. The goal was not to "save souls" but to be in partnership with those in the community. In the US, most urban work was undertaken by seminaries and was academically oriented (the strong exception being the East Harlem Protestant Parish of Union Theological School). While study is important at UTU, the orientation is to praxis. A more mundane reason, but one that had sway with church authorities, was that it was less expensive to go to Sheffield than to do anything with a US seminary! From my perspective, it was important to take people out of their comfort zone, disorient them somewhat, with the goal of making them more open to new ideas. Throughout the seven years of the program, most participants had never been outside the United States, many never outside New England. Most people were open to seeing with new eyes, hearing with new ears, and acting with a new focus. There were, of course, those who kept minds and vision firmly shut, and those settings faded from the scene—and often the churches faded into history.

It was characteristic of John to emphasize several recurring themes: Christianity as discipleship; theology as reflection on discipleship in particular places, shared lay and ordained agendas for missions, among others. John didn't so much expect us to take it all on board but to be provoked in a distinctive way of practice.

In the second year, churches were to undertake their chosen project, evaluating with the others in their group every three months. John returned at the end of this period to review and evaluate all of the projects. He was sometimes very charitable! But, for the most part, churches plunged in and did the work. It was much like the sower, one of John's favorite stories: some grew mightily with a great harvest, others flared up—and out—and a few just wilted.

Over the course of the next seven years, some forty settings, not all churches, participated with varied results, but all grateful to John for his direction and inspiration. Twenty years on, most of the pastors have retired, but many ministries continue. One pastor who has not yet retired is Gary Richards, who was serving a tiny church in western Massachusetts, whose church made significant gains in mission and witness in the community during the very first experience. Gary went on to work in several urban settings. He pastored a multiracial congregation in Worcester, Massachusetts, leading them to a collaboration with one of the local colleges and planting a community garden. His next parish was also multiracial, this time with members from Ghana, rather than Latino, in East Hartford, Connecticut, helping that congregation come to terms with its changing community using UTU methodology. Gary is now senior pastor at an interesting outer-urban setting involving two massive buildings built at the turn of the twentieth century, in Belmont and Watertown, Massachusetts, the latter being a church I had served in the 1980s before going into administration.

Belmont is the much larger congregation, though Watertown houses a Korean congregation for which Gary has nominal responsibility. The Belmont church is in dire need of major repair, and usually a church of that size and wealth would put up the money and devote itself to survival. Under Gary's leadership, they have decided to sell the Belmont building, renovate Watertown, and move all ministry there. This is a major decision for any congregation, but especially one that is cognizant of its prestige and standing. Gary helped them see the true meaning of ministry and service and attributes his understanding of missional ministry to John Vincent.

Stories of Remnants

Since John is given to teaching through stories, there is one more that I should add, one that strikes closer to home. At the end of the nineties, while I was superintendent for southern Maine, Sue, my wife, began attending a historic church in Portland, Maine, Chestnut St., the "mother church" for Maine. Owing to urban development, what had once been its neighborhood was now a highway, and the church which had numbered close to one thousand was now down to a few dozen, rattling around in an ark of a building. Sue, too, is a disciple of John's, having worked with him at a conference in Hawarden and knowing him over several years. She gathered a group at Chestnut St. for Bible study, leading to some dramatic conclusions about the future of the church, and had almost persuaded the leadership to send a delegation to Sheffield to work with John. This plan was kiboshed by some who would not face the reality of the situation and saw what Sue and the group were doing as too radical. (John would be pleased!)

A year later, the church had to close, and Sue was by then chair of the trustees. She managed the sale of the building to an empathetic developer and worked with the pastor and a remnant to continue ministry. They went into a local synagogue and began their discernment. They were joined by a remnant from another closing church in a neighboring town. Sue then began a new Bible study, based, naturally, on Mark. We maintained contact with John and Grace.

After about three years, working with two interim ministers, a pastoral team was appointed in 2007 by the bishop. Allen and Sara Ewing Merrill were thought by the conference to be starting a new church and getting rid of the old folks at the synagogue, of whom there were about twenty. But they, by this time "we," as I was now retired, refused to die off, so Allen and Sara were essentially serving two congregations, which was both absurd and beneficial. While neither could be self-sustaining, the advantage of separation is that it allowed the young congregation, many of whom were unchurched previously or had had bad experiences with the organized church (primarily over issues of sexuality, gender, or authoritarianism), to develop new models for leadership. As we moved toward creating a single "new" congregation, we persuaded Allen and Sara, with their one-year-old daughter and two laypersons, to go to Sheffield for a week and work with John.

The effect was transformative. They returned with creative ideas and a renewed vision of what was possible for Portland. The most important concept, though it appears far from radical, is that you welcome anyone who comes in and work with them. We described it as "kissing anyone who comes in." The first such visitors were those in addiction recovery. We became the home for many of those recovering and for years housed several addiction recovery groups. That tie ended only with COVID restrictions and perhaps will resume in the future.

The second group were asylum seekers from Burundi. In a short time, we formed a "Friends of Burundi" group, assisting in legal issues, housing, and a small level of financial support. Soon, however, our Burundi ministry was being criticized by those from Rwanda, and we recognized the need to expand our horizons. We now have, in addition to those ethnic groups,

Angolans, Congolese from the DCR, and a few other individuals from various other African countries—despite the relatively cold weather!

The congregation, now HopeGateWay, is in its second storefront, having outgrown the first. The congregation is multiracial and multinational, with asylum seekers from Central Africa playing a large part. Until COVID, there were two services on Sunday, with about one hundred in worship, and we looked forward to getting back into in-person worship by Easter 2022. In 2002, Allen and a team of eight of us, responding to the needs of both Africans and addiction-challenged folk, created Hope Acts as a nonprofit offshoot to do diverse forms of ministry and to attract secular funding. Hope Acts became a stand-alone charity a couple years later, having been given a disused Lutheran church to use as an intermediate home for thirteen asylum seekers. The donor of the building was the same person whom Sue worked with to sell Chestnut St. and who was impressed with the ministry at HGW. He attends a progressive Episcopal church. Today, Hope Acts is recognized in Portland as one of the leading organizations in Portland working with new Mainers. In addition to housing thirteen asylum seekers, we work with several hundred annually to get work permits, deal with immigration issues, and find housing. The English as a Second Language program has about seventy-five persons and works with Portland Adult Education to bring the skills and resources of these new Mainers into the mainstream of Maine life. COVID made such work even more difficult, but the work of Martha Stein, the executive director, and of her part-time staff has been incredible and raised Hope Acts's profile in Portland.

Hope Acts began with some funds left from the sale of Chestnut St., about $140,000, enough to furnish Hope House and to have Allen as part-time executive director and one very part-time administrative aide. With Martha, we have six part-time employees, half of whom are themselves new Mainers, several interns from other agencies or local colleges, and a budget of $350,000. Though independent, there is still a strong relationship between HopeGateWay and Hope Acts. Two of us from HGW continue to sit on the Hope Acts board, and the emphasis continues to be flexibility and openness to new forms of ministry, though we don't call it that in public, as we are now a "secular" charity.

A new chapter in the life HopeGateWay is now being written, as the congregation has disaffiliated from the United Methodist Church over the denomination's appalling rules regarding the LGBTQ community. We have been criticized for not staying and fighting for a fuller understanding of our common humanity, but it has been fifty years since the United Methodist Church passed its first exclusionary legislation with regard to LGBTQ persons, and legislation has become only more punitive, such that of the eighteen clergy who worship at HGW, mostly retired, more than half of us would be subject to sanctions and even unfrocking for having performed same-sex marriages. That wouldn't happen in our relatively progressive conference, but we are still considered by the "Pharisees" to be "unclean."

We continue to believe that ministry is more important than institutions, in keeping with the way of Jesus, and we continue to seek ways to live out the Gospel of Mark, remaining true to guidance given by John Vincent.

Rev. Don Rudalevige

14

John's Contribution to Ministerial Training

Christine Jones

It was against a changing background in Methodism about ministerial training that John Vincent's vision of Methodist ministerial students training at UTU was to become a reality.[1] If the connexion was asking questions about providing appropriate training for its ministers, then UTU was the ideal place to train people to work in an urban environment. John's conviction that discipleship involved a journey downward had the potential to become an integral part of those training for such ministry. Changes in

---

1. Traditionally, Methodist ministerial training was delivered through a small number of residential colleges, usually over a three- to four-year period, and when the numbers training were considerably higher than they are currently. Conference was presented with various options, one of which was definitively rejected, that is, to place a cap on the number of those accepted for training each year. Nevertheless, the fact that such a suggestion had been made provided the opportunity to ask deeper questions relating to the overall aims of ministerial training. In some quarters there was a real desire for a better quality of training, including the belief that there ought to be an emphasis on formation and more objective criteria for selection. The report provided the opportunity to ask, "What are we training people for: What training is necessary to produce the ministers who are needed as the church enters the twenty-first century?" It was not only the Methodist Church that was struggling with these issues. The same problems and questions were also being experienced ecumenically, and these shared challenges became part of the solution as Methodist ministerial training started to be offered in regional centers. Here, Methodists trained with those of other denominations, often Anglicans, but Manchester, for example, included Methodists, Baptists, URC, and Unitarians. I am grateful to the Rev. Ken Howcroft for the conversations that provided much background information for this note.

connexional policy made the 1990s an ideal time for John's dream to come to fruition.

If there were positive changes happening in Methodism, there were more challenging changes taking place in our relationship with the universities. Although, for whatever reason, we never had a church review, there were plenty of university appraisals, most of which contained various degrees of stress and all of which produced a considerable amount of extra work for everyone involved. If the story of ministerial training at UTU is to be told, then a brief explanation of our relationship with different universities is inescapable. When I was first appointed as director of studies, following Inderjit Bhogal, who had become director of UTU in 1997 following John's retirement, our modules were validated by the University of Sheffield thanks largely to John's negotiations with Professor John Rogerson, head of the Biblical Studies Department.

A Changing Educational Environment

In the early years of the new millennium, things changed. Rather than our relationship with the university depending on the Biblical Studies Department, a new department that looked after "off-site centers" (the Board of Collegiate Studies) was set up, and it was made clear that radical changes were to be made, including the administration of the courses that were taught. Despite criticisms being leveled at us about our procedures not being up to date, I can remember one of our external examiners, who had worked in Methodist ministerial training for many years, saying after one exam board, he had never before seen a cohort of students with such consistently high standards.

Following our initial encounters with the new board at the university, Jan Royan and I often worked late into the evening writing, and then rewriting, handbooks for each module we taught, as one of the criticisms was that these did not yet exist. In retrospect, some of the challenges made were fair ones, but some of the meetings held with the university felt unfriendly and unsupportive, and, ultimately, we were told we were losing our validation, along with all the off-site centers they looked after. This was a difficult period, maybe especially for John, who had brokered the initial relationship. The decision by the university could have put our ability to provide ministerial training at risk: if we could not provide students with a degree, then we would not receive ministerial students. Following those initial encounters with the Board of Collegiate Studies, some of us anticipated we would lose our validation, though I think John believed longer than I did that all would be well. For the staff, this was a difficult time, feeling that our opportunity to provide ministerial training hung in the balance, and after long discussions it was agreed that we needed to explore alternative options.

At the time, Jan Royan was studying for an MA at York St. John and knew the staff there; in addition, the York Institute had recently been set up, and I had met with Rev. James Jones to talk about ways in which the students from the respective institutions might share things like the annual retreat. These relationships formed the basis of our negotiations with York St. John, and in a relatively short space of time it was agreed they would provide our validation. As they taught only an MA (validated by Leeds University), it meant that rather than teaching modules for UTU's bachelor of ministry and theology (BMinTheol), we quickly had to adapt to teaching a new set of modules and seeing if any of our previous modules were similar enough to theirs. We quickly developed a good working relationship with York St. John, including, in partnership with others, writing new modules for the new foundation degree course which eventually most of our ministerial students registered for.

John's Influence on the Curriculum and Classroom

Working with Inderjit Bhogal, I had done some voluntary teaching with the ministerial students prior to my appointment as director of studies in 1997, the year John retired. This meant that in the first year, I saw very little of John, but his influence was still present in terms of the modules that were being taught. As stated above, the BMinTheol modules were validated by the University of Sheffield and were basically the material previously used on the study year and included introductions to doing urban theology and liberation theology. Since those initial days, the validating university changed more than once, which meant writing new modules or adapting to ones already approved by the universities, so what we taught when is no longer as clear as it could be!

From a connexional perspective, UTU remained unique in the mix of centers and colleges that provided ministerial training. I remember submitting programs outlining what was being taught, and although we consistently avoided formal inspections and reviews, we did fit into the new approach and ethos of ministerial training. Part of John's conviction, of being rooted in the communities in which we serve, reflected almost exactly, though probably expressed in different language, what the connexion was hoping to achieve in relation to ministerial training. The aim of both was to provide minsters with the skills to analyze and understand the communities they would find themselves in and to identify God's presence in those contexts. UTU had become an ideal place for ministerial training

John's passion, apart from Mark's Gospel, is his conviction that theology must be more than an academic subject; it needs to be based on people's experience and an analysis of their context. John was a "powerful voice" advocating the importance of contextual theology, liberation theology, urban theology, and reflective practice: UTU might not have been the only place to include these subjects, but the emphasis John gave to these areas of theology meant UTU was possibly the only place where these subjects influenced the whole curriculum, including the way students were taught and encouraged to practice ministry.[2]

As someone who read theology in the late 1960s to early 1970s, I was used to approaching the text from a historical-critical perspective and engaging in close textual analysis. I found my first introduction to liberation and contextual theology extremely challenging and initially was critical of the whole approach. But, having started my own ministry, I was soon finding that the traditional approach was very far removed from the lives and ideas of the people whom I encountered and was trying to work with. I had never been taught to relate text to context, which, it seemed to me, was an increasingly important thing to be able to do, and I was starting to find the answers in liberation and feminist theology. I can't say, as Laurie Green does, that John was the person who inspired me to change my theological perspectives, but I do realize that working with John and others at UTU reinforced my understanding that ministry needs to be about a social and political awareness that will challenge injustice and the wrongs within our society, and that the biblical texts regularly support that understanding. If ministerial formation is about resourcing people to work in different contexts, then their preparation for ministry needs to include acquiring the tools for contextual, social, and political analysis, and a textual hermeneutic that supports that. I think it is largely due to John's influence that I was able to at least start doing that.

---

2. I am grateful to Ken Howcroft for this quote and the insights reflected here.

My PhD dissertation was entitled "The Reformation of Formation" (University of Nottingham). As part of the research, I interviewed a number of students, some from UTU but also others who were attending or had recently attended some of the other training centers. Now is not the place to explain that in any detail, but there is one important aspect that again relates back to John's positive influence. It is important to say that I think the situation has changed considerably since this research was completed; but then, sadly, more than half of the students I interviewed had struggled with their time in training. Some had felt bullied by other students, and they and others complained of feeling unsupported by staff.

When asked whether they felt their formation as a minister had taken place, those who felt they had not received positive pastoral care all gave a negative response. I could not claim that every student sent to UTU for training was completely happy or satisfied; there were high expectations of the students but also a high level of informality. There was no formal classroom, as we met in the front room of 210 Abbeyfield Road and encouraged honest questioning and debate. Students were challenged, but there was also the understanding that these people, currently our students, could easily become our colleagues in a future circuit.

Part of the aim, even when asking challenging questions, was to provide a safe space: a place in which people felt confident to ask difficult questions, express different opinions, but to always do so with respect. I think perhaps John and I both wanted to provide that space where people could discuss honestly and openly, though perhaps approached how to do so in a slightly different way.

As I've already said, the course offered to ministerial students changed during the years I was at UTU. Some of those changes caused a great deal of soul-searching and anxiety, but I found that when those changes could be justified, John was always helpful, supportive, and a dependable colleague. One of the things that I enjoyed doing was being allowed to create new modules, and on one occasion I shared with John an idea for a new module that was to be called "The Bible and the City."[3] Ultimately, the module was accepted and became part of the suite of modules studied by those in ministerial training. John Rogerson and John Vincent shared some of the

---

3. He was genuinely pleased that, unknown to me, this coincided with a project he was working on with Professor John Rogerson, which became a joint book: Rogerson and Vincent, *City in Biblical Perspective*.

teaching, while I did the less exciting parts of the course, making sure the learning outcomes were fulfilled and the assignment titles understood.

It was a privilege to be present in those sessions: both men so passionate about their subject; both sharing their experience and their knowledge and discussing points about which they agreed and sometimes disagreed; both easily sidetracked by questions and using those queries to develop inclusive, challenging conversations in which students learned far more than could be found in the stated aims of the course.

Searching for Validation (Again)

While the "Making of Ministry Report" from the Methodist Conference of 1997 had provided a positive background for UTU to offer ministerial training, the "Connexional Training Strategies" report sadly led to its ultimate demise, along with other colleges that ceased to provide this training following the massive reorganization undertaken by the Methodist Church.[4] UTU's uniqueness in having at the basis of its program a combination of urban, contextual, and liberation theology seemed to give way to the need for larger cohorts and the desire, where possible, to work ecumenically—a challenge leveled against us I found difficult, as our staff were a model of ecumenism. For example, Debbie Herring, who taught a number of the academic modules taken by the ministerial students, was an Anglican. York St. John (which had become a university in its own right) was, by this time, providing ministerial training for the Anglican priesthood, and it became necessary for us, on occasion, to share modules with them, which was not always entirely satisfactory, as the structures and practices of the two churches vary considerably. The report also required us to work more closely with the York Institute, so in effect the two cohorts came together. It was not long before UTU was called to a meeting at the university to be told that we would be losing their validation mostly because of the number of students that we had at any one time. So, again, the search began for validation elsewhere.

As one of the main parts of my job at UTU had been working with ministerial students, and because I had suffered some prolonged periods of serious ill health, which I know (because we worked with a small team) made it difficult for the rest of the staff, who never complained and gave

---

4. Trustees for Methodist Church Purposes: "Making of Ministry Report"; "Connexional Training Strategies."

great support, sadly I decided to leave UTU at the end of the 2010 academic year.

I had been external examiner at Luther King House Manchester and had been appointed as tutor for their church-related community workers starting in September 2010, and that is where my story relating to ministerial training at UTU needs to end, as colleagues began negotiation with Luther King House to be validated with Manchester University through them; and eventually UTU became a constituent college of Luther King Educational Trust. It is also at this point that ministerial training at UTU dramatically changed, and my involvement in ministerial training as part of UTU's story ended.

Although Methodist ministerial training was not always a part of UTU's life, I like to think that it had an impact on those who trained with us and on wider Methodism. Often, in relation to ministerial training, John was a figure in the background, but his influence, his commitment to community engagement and finding God in our own contexts, his desire to remove theology from the "ivory towers" into real life, lay at the heart of ministerial training at UTU; and for that I and, I think, many others are grateful.

Rev. Dr. Christine Jones: UTU director of studies (1997–2004), director (2004–10)

Bibliography

Jones, Christine. "A Reformation of Formation: A Critique of Methodist Ministerial Training." PhD diss., University of Nottingham, 2009.

Rogerson, J. W., and John J. Vincent. *The City in Biblical Perspective*. Biblical Challenges in the Contemporary World. London: Routledge, 2014.

Trustees for Methodist Church Purposes, eds. "Connexional Training Strategies: Implementing the Making of Ministry Report and Concept 2000." In *Methodist Conference Scarborough (18th–26th June 1998)*, 2:591–609. Peterborough, UK: Methodist, 2000.

———. "Making of Ministry Report." In *Methodist Conference 1997 (25th June to 5th July 1997)*, 1:209–27. Peterborough, UK: Methodist, 2000.

15

Emmaus Road in Birmingham: Galilee in Sheffield

Ruth Weston

I HAD AN EMMAUS Road experience myself. Not with Jesus Christ but with the Rev. Dr. John Vincent. As a young theological postgraduate in 1990, I was reading a lot of Vincent's theology and work; and by way of this, the Methodist chaplain of my university got me an invite to a conference where John was speaking. It occurred just before the Easter term began, and so one cold, wet January afternoon, I got off the train at Birmingham University station staggering with my two suitcases and a rucksack. I asked the nearest person where the chaplaincy might be, and the man said that he knew and, picking up one of my cases, said that as he was going in that direction, he would take me there. A third man overhearing us said he was going to the same place and, picking up my other suitcase, asked if he could come with us. And so, we set off. Our guide asked me what brought me to the university, and I explained it was to hear a theologian whom I had read much of and admired. I returned the question to my guide, who answered that he worked at the university.

Recognizing the Stranger

Then we turned to our companion: "Who are you?" And with a sparkle in his eye, he said, "I am John Vincent!" And then I saw that it was! I had seen his photo on the back of each of his books so I knew what he looked like, but I really had not then believed such a great theologian might be getting off a train to walk in the rain to a conference! And because I had not believed it possible, I had not seen what was before my very eyes! The Emmaus Road story came alive for me then—with that ring of truth that comes from personal experience, and I have been telling the tale in my Easter sermons ever since.

So, what did John Vincent do for me, and how did he change my life? By the Sea of Galilee with its wide horizons I learned both discipleship and my craft at the Urban Theology Unit under the tutelage of John Vincent. My Galilee was not the blue waters of a Near Eastern sea but the seven hills of Sheffield, inner-city Sheffield, where poverty and deprivation were endemic.

As John does, he convinced me that I should do the study year in Sheffield, which I did, starting at the beginning of 1991. It was a very difficult year on a personal level, and it took some years to process the learning there to be applied, but I was hooked on doing this grounded, living theology that John both taught and embodied. And although I wandered far beyond Galilee, the tools, the skills, the attitude I learned there have remained: working out how to live the radical gospel in the places and situations I am in and seeking to strategically place myself in the places where the gospel happens.

A Testament: It Happened Like This

And where did the gospel happen? It took some years to work this out, partly because I did not recognize what was before my eyes—even as I carried one baby after another to UTU each year! Where I worked out my discipleship was in the family home and the toddler groups of Bradford; and I took the radical gospel I had learned at UTU into the maternity system and mothering communities there. And like my Emmaus Road experience, if not more so, the moment of revelation, of grace, of choice was as cataclysmic as the moment Jesus addressed Zacchaeus in the tree, or as Levi left his counting table, or Peter walked away from his fishing nets. The story goes like this:

In 2002, eight weeks before the birth of my fourth child, I rang to book the hire of my birthing pool from a Leeds-based midwife.

"I am sorry, I can't," came the response. "I will be in New Zealand in three weeks' time."

"Is this for a holiday?" I asked slowly.

"No. I am emigrating. Leaving in three weeks."
"So what will happen to the pools?"
"The pools and the business are for sale."
"Can I hire a pool off the person buying it?"
"No one is buying the business."
"Oh." Long pause.
"So what will happen to the pools?"
"At this stage? I will just leave them in the garage."

And the community activist in me thought: if she leaves the pools in the garage, I won't be able to have my water birth, but neither will women all over Yorkshire—except at London prices shipped up here, and we would not want that!

"I'll take it on." I said. Just like that.

"Really?"

"Yes," I said. Thinks. Then: "Oh! I had better ask my husband." I rang my husband at work and said, "Sit down. Because you'll never guess what I've just done!"

"The washing machine has broken."

"No. It's not that—I've bought a business—I have just bought the pool hire company—that's okay, isn't it?"

To my surprise, he was really pleased for me. This was good, because it was his money.

By some miracle, my parents turned up an hour later unannounced, on their way home from somewhere. I told them what I had just done. I was surprised by how pleased they were! This was good, because I was a community organizer—I could set up projects and campaigns, but I had never set up or run a business before.

That was Friday. On Tuesday, we agreed terms on the train to work. On Thursday, we went over after work and kids' teatime, where we were given a box full of files and viewed the pools in the garage by flashlight. It was then she told us she had got an earlier flight and she was leaving on Sunday for her new life. That was it. We were the new owners of Aquabirths Birthing Pools on July 5, 2002, ten days after ringing up to hire a birth pool and six weeks before the birth of my fourth child.

This was the call: to leave the counting table and the fishing nets and follow where the radical gospel led. This was the point when my work life/sense of vocation collided and became one with my role as a mother. The personal became political, and I also meant business, because it was my living—my business. This was the moment when I threw in the towel and said: Okay—I will do this! You have called me to live the radical gospel here: I will become a birth activist rather than a generic community organizer. Change making not in the church or the community generally but in maternity with moms and midwives and the gamut of maternity life. And I think God smiled, because a force of nature had been unleashed upon an unsuspecting world!

Anyway, I completed the diploma in theology and ministry at UTU in 1994 and continued to attend courses at UTU for many years. The theology John taught and embodied rendered me unemployable, but I succeeded in having five children, becoming a social entrepreneur running several maternity businesses, and being a well-known birth activist both locally in West Yorkshire and nationally. I now live in rural Wales but maintain my vocation as a guerrilla activist.

Apocalyptic Outbursts

John Vincent in personal conversations and in the form of the UTU unfolded for me a kind of rigorous theology that you did rather than read. At UTU, returning again and again over many years, I learned how to *do* theology in my context. I learned so much at UTU, and it has become so embedded in my activism that it is sometimes difficult to unearth it. And yet, I have particular memories of things at UTU and what John said that have stayed with me over the years.

For example, I remember one of John's outbursts—and they could feel like outbursts even if they were not—where John told us that if you wanted to work in the urban context and grassroots level then you had better get used to failure. Failure is the norm, he told us. In the same talk he talked about being a social entrepreneur: to make any change happen, we had to be creative, inventive, and entrepreneurial, mainly because powerless people do not have a seat at the decision-making table nor money to buy it. In the years as a community organizer and maternity activist in West Yorkshire, this teaching has resonated so many times, enabling me not to take failure personally but to think about how to do it differently next time to get the result needed. I think that if some NHS mangers had known where I had learned my craft, they would have had John assassinated.

What has stayed in my mind over the decades, keeping me in check and self-aware, is two gatherings: one of Black theologians and leaders, and another of disability theologians and leaders. Here, we were not participants but observers, representing the White and hearing societies that had destructively discriminated against and indeed enslaved the people we were listening to. We sat and listened. And I learned something of what it feels like to be Black in a White-dominated church and society, and to live with a hearing disability in a hearing world. But I also learned what it feels like to be a privileged or powerful person held to account: it taught me what it might feel like to be the consultant, the head of midwifery, the commissioner on the end of one of our challenges. It taught me to stand in the shoes of others and see the world through their eyes. It taught me to find ways to build allies out of people who would otherwise be opponents. It taught me so much just by being there with ears and heart open, and mouth shut.

And, finally, the resonant phrase "soft underbelly of the oppressive state" remains as uncomfortable to hear now as when John said it. It has been equally uncomfortable for the midwives I have taught. Whatever John said at the time, it has been the phrase I have used to describe the work of good health-care professionals locked into the maternity system. They mitigate cruel policies and guidelines with kind words and ameliorate painful practices with subversive acts. This kindness is important; however, we must be clear what it is and what it does and its limitations: it makes bearable and acceptable policies and practice that are neither acceptable nor ethical. By doing so it shores up a patriarchal and hierarchical system that is damaging to the lives of women and babies. Ultimately the system should be brought to account and made to work for those it is supposed to serve—women and their families.

As I became immersed in the mission I had been given, my visits to UTU became infrequent and stopped altogether. Sent out, I had left Galilee behind to take the gospel to the ends of the earth. But after many years absence from UTU, I have circled back to where I began. True to the liberation hermeneutic I studied and practiced, I now reflect on what I have done and write it up. There is nowhere else I would go to do this. The results, as they say, will be found in all good bookstores in due course: *Born Stroppy: Make Change Happen*!

John and the Urban Theology Unit he formed gave me a theological framework to seek and discover discipleship, not where it was needed but where it was needed most. He taught me practical skills, shared experience and insight, mentored and guided, put me in the way of people and experiences that altered my attitudes and challenged my assumptions. He tore up the anodyne gospel I had been fed and gave back to me a gospel that was compelling, difficult and adventurous, which ruined my career (the journey downward) but helped me make a real difference in people's lives. And like him, I am now compelled to pass it on, because discipleship does not stop; it just changes.

Ruth Weston: UTU graduate, Dip. Theol. Min. (1994), birth activist, author

Bibliography

Weston, Ruth. *Born Stroppy: Make Change Happen*. London: Book Brilliance, 2025.

PART VI

The Primacy of Radical Christianity

Introduction

Orientation to the Primacy of Radical Christianity

Ian K. Duffield

John talks about "changing the world from the bottom" because the gospel practice on which he is focused and the discipleship to which he calls concerns those in the urban who are neglected or undervalued or oppressed, and he sees in them the key to moving forward. In this, John is within the tradition and trajectory of historical radical Christianity evidenced by *Radical Christian Writings: A Reader*, edited by Andrew Bradstock and Chris Rowland, which includes an extract from John's book *O.K., Let's Be Methodists*.[1] This radicalism started very early on: John was involved in the formation of the Methodist Renewal Group in 1960; and the desire to develop the Methodist radical witness led to the formation of the Alliance of Radical Methodists in May 1971 with a biannual publication, which continued until 2004. It also explains John and UTU's more recent involvement in and support for the St. Mark's Centre for Radical Christianity, founded in Sheffield, which provided a platform, for example, for John and Ken Leech, and brought Marcus Borg and John Dominic Crossan, with their radical takes on Jesus, to Britain. John's radicalism is evident from start to finish.

Such radicalism is about the radical, the roots, and for him it is what he often refers to as "the bottom" and that this is a propitious place to begin, contrary to normal expectations: "The gospel of incarnation is always about

---

1. Vincent, "O.K., Let's Be Methodists."

Introduction to Part VI

what happens 'at the bottom.'"[2] In this, of course, he is at one with liberation theology in beginning with the poor and seeing theology, discipleship, and gospel action as emerging from the poor—the poor not seen as a class to be pitied but people among whom to live and work, hence John's lifetime of living in the Burngreave area on the wrong side of Sheffield and the deliberate choice of title for the Methodist program that John invented: "Mission Alongside the Poor." And for John this is how the world is changed: "from the bottom up," not "from the top down," which is a characteristic, even if not always expressed, of radical Christianity throughout the centuries. So, it was easy for UTU to make use of liberation theology because it so chimed with John's original vision. How urban theology, which is John's creation, relates to liberation theology and contextual theology was explored by John, Christine Jones, and myself in *Crucibles: Creating Theology at UTU*, which was our attempt to explain to the academy what we thought we were about and how what UTU did correlated with those other movements.[3]

There's no doubt that John and liberation theology and the tradition of radical Christianity influenced Robin Pagan and me when we began our lifetime writing project on developing a radical interpretation of the biblical text, which had the embryonic title: "Radical Voices on the Bible." Although John focuses on Mark and the liberationists have their favorite passages, we were inspired to contemplate and dared to believe that if Jesus was radical and the Bible was radical,[4] it was possible to interpret every scriptural passage in a radical/liberational way. Initially, we envisaged only collating the interpretations of John and the liberation theologians and the like (e.g., Black, feminist, and social readings) as a handy resource; but it soon developed into our own commentary on the text, not least because we often could not find a sufficiently radical interpretation in the literature, so we were forced to engage in it ourselves.[5]

2. Vincent, *Strategies for Mission*, 2.

3. Duffield et al., *Crucibles*. I've also written on their interrelation in *Faithfulness in the City*; and on the way the research that has taken place at UTU may be seen in this light, see my "Radical Christianity in Research."

4. See Desmond Tutu's famous affirmation: "The Bible is the most revolutionary, the most radical book there is" (Tutu, *Hope and Suffering*, 178).

5. Although we have done work on every book of the Bible, we have inevitably focused on the Synoptic Gospels and the Jesus tradition; not surprisingly, the title of our unpublished magnum opus is "A Radical Commentary—the First Three Gospels." We deal with the gospel narrative synoptically and have divided it into seven sections, the titles of which indicate our approach: 1. God's Radical Prophet; 2. Jesus' Radical Torah; 3. Jesus' Liberational Practice; 4. Jesus' Provocative Speech; 5. Jesus' Marginal Living; 6.

Introduction to Part VI

Whether others regard us as radical, or radical enough, is a question for them, but there is no question in our mind about this lifetime project, which grew out of our friendship and colleagueship at UTU. For us, it is testimony to the creative influence of John and UTU. There is no way that this project would have ever taken off otherwise. It testifies to the power of a radical reading of Scripture that is never ending; but we have found it a fruitful resource for our own thinking and practice and hope for the publication of the whole volume in the near future. So, for me, the influence of John and the impact of UTU have helped shape my life in ministry. They're how I ended up in Sheffield and have been here ever since; they help to explain my ministry in an urban village and on two of the most deprived council housing estates in Sheffield (Manor and Southey Green) on different sides of the city. They help to explain how I moved from systematic theology (which was the focus of my MTh at King's London) to contextual biblical interpretation, and from suburban ministry in the leafy suburbs of St. Alban's Diocese to urban ministry in Sheffield Diocese (which was the focus of my DMin). They help to explain how I moved from lecturing on Colossians and Christology to working with people on developing urban ministry projects (and Church Urban Fund projects) and to supervising doctoral work, often on the front line of ministry.

If Anglicanism is something of a head religion (think Richard Hooker; William Temple), and Roman Catholicism is something of a hand religion (think the rosary, making the sign of the cross; what the French composer Francis Poulenc affirmed as "rustic devotion"), and Methodism/Pentecostalism is something of a heart religion (think of Wesley's heart being strangely warmed or of Pentecostal fervor), then John's radical approach is distinct because it's something of a feet religion—where we are, where our feet are, determines who we are and how we think, and points to whom we're with (e.g., alongside the poor), and indicates action, practice (and, of course, John prefers to view Wesley as within this trajectory). So John calls people to urban discipleship and to the doing of alternatives, to gospel practice in the secular world. Not surprisingly, this coheres with the Christian radical tradition. So, the one who points to and follows the radical Jesus enters the mysteries of Jesus and becomes the radical disciple: John J. Vincent.

Jesus' Prophetic Actions; 7. Jesus' Radical Resistance.

Introduction to Part VI

Bibliography

Duffield, Ian K. "Urban Theology: Location, Vocation, Action." In *Faithfulness in the City*, edited by John J. Vincent, 266–79. New York: Monad, 2003.

———. "Radical Christianity in Research." In *Radical Christianity: Roots and Fruits*, edited by Chris Rowland and John Vincent, 96–104. British Liberation Theology 6. Sheffield: UTU, 2016.

Duffield, Ian K., and Robin Pagan. "A Radical Commentary—the First Three Gospels." Unpublished manuscript, last modified 2023. Microsoft Word file.

Duffield, Ian K., et al. *Crucibles: Creating Theology at UTU*. New City Special 14. Sheffield: UTU, 2000.

Tutu, Desmond. *Hope and Suffering: Sermons and Speeches*. London: Fount, 1984.

Vincent, John J. "O.K., Let's Be Methodists." In *Radical Christian Writings: A Reader*, edited by Andrew Bradstock and Christopher Rowland, 280–84. Oxford: Blackwell, 1984.

———. *Strategies for Mission*. Sheffield: UTU, 1977.

16

A Journey of Theological Self-Discovery

Joe Aldred

In her book *When God Calls*, Dianne Sealey-Skerritt discusses God interventions and shows how, in her experience, God calls us on a journey, a divine quest for justice and fairness.[1] In this symbiotic God/human relationship, divine intervention is at work so that, as my Pentecostal upbringing has taught me, there are only God-incidences, no coincidences. This sense of the ontologically Divine One, simultaneously transcendent and immanent, runs in my African beingness, expressed as John Mbiti suggests in the Ashanti proverb, "No one shows a child the Supreme Being."[2] Notwithstanding this truism, my mother showed me God anthropomorphically through her own faith in One who is the causation in one's life, directing, providing, sustaining, pastoring, healing, and saving.[3] It was a God-driven journey from Top Mountain, St. Catherine, Jamaica, that brought me to Sheffield, England, in the summer of 1989, as I describe in my autobiography *From Top Mountain*.

Shortly after our arriving in Sheffield in 1989 to begin my ministry in the region as pastor and area bishop, a handwritten note came through our letter box. The note read something like this, "Dear Joe, I have been told I should invite you to the Urban Theology Unit. Can you make it on (date) at (time)?" It was signed, "Yours, John." At the time I knew of neither John nor UTU. And to this day I do not know who suggested John extend the

---

1. Sealey-Skerritt, *When God Calls*, 79.
2. Mbiti, *African Religions and Philosophy*, 29.
3. Mbiti, *African Religions and Philosophy*, 43.

invitation to me. Thus began a relationship from which I have benefited disproportionately, for which I will be forever thankful. Two 70,000-word theses later, a master of ministry and theology with distinction in 1994—"A Black-Majority Church's Future"—and a PhD in 2004—"Respect: A Caribbean British Theology," published as *Respect: Understanding Caribbean British Christianity*—and three decades since our first meeting, John remains a transformative figure of immense influence in my life and ministry, for which I will forever be in his debt. I welcome this opportunity to put on record my appreciation for John and the phenomenon called UTU he gave birth to.

A Radical Like Jesus . . . in Birmingham, Manchester, and Sheffield

The radicality of the urban Jesus at the epicenter of John's theological philosophy was in stark contrast to the pious, otherworldly Jesus of my Pentecostal upbringing in which a pneumatic Holy Spirit was central. Jesus up until the UTU encounter was mediator of my personal salvation, celebrated in the Sunday worship experience but quickly superseded by the experience of being "filled with the Spirit" and consumed by its "fire."[4]

For John, Christianity is about Jesus and the liberation and empowerment of poor urban people, a theme captured beautifully by a fellow Pentecostal UTU student, the national overseer of the New Testament Church of God, Selwyn E. Arnold, in his resulting work, *From Scepticism to Hope*: Jesus was and is at work in the world, therefore followers of Jesus should be at work in the world. Like Jesus was in first-century Palestine, so we should be now in Birmingham, Manchester, and Sheffield. As John puts it in *Radical Jesus*: this Jesus "walks the streets, creates my communities, freaks out my neighbours, judges my friends, calls my enemies, offends my fellow ministers, heals my sick neighbours, breaks into my world views, exposes my betrayals."[5] John challenged the tradition of my upbringing's smug satisfaction in being "saved, sanctified and filled in the Holy Ghost," with being a disciple of the Jesus found in the gospels, particularly for John, Mark's Gospel. John's Jesus is much more than the baptizer in the Holy Spirit as an end in itself, but rather the purveyor and architect of new possibilities,

---

4. For a history of early Pentecostalism, see Anderson, *Spreading Fires*.
5. Vincent, *Radical Jesus*, 7.

bringing something innovative and new into situations, providing ways for a person to move, to change, to discover, to revolutionize.[6]

To encounter John was to enter a whirlwind of mature excitableness and seemingly endless possibilities to explore Jesus's ideas, to discover and rediscover Jesus of the gospels. This is the Jesus whose radicality calls followers to get to the roots of things, undeterred by the attempt at denominational capture of the Jesus follower's gaze. This is the Jesus who is a radical, not a revolutionary who seeks achievable changes after which all will be well, not a liberal, a revisionist, or an enlightener manipulating sociological theories; not a fundamentalist or literalist, but a radical pointing away from himself toward God's kingdom, calling for radical followers.[7] For me, UTU was a space to develop or reformulate one's theology and vocation in pursuit of this radical discipleship.[8]

Black Incarnation

Before attending UTU, I had already completed in-house denominational studies in my US-based international Pentecostal church. In addition, Old and New Testament biblical studies at St. John's Nottingham by remote learning had began the task of introducing me to academic theological and biblical studies. But it was the liberating learning space of UTU, accredited by Sheffield University, that facilitated the freedom to explore who I was as a follower of Jesus and what I had been taught and embraced. With freedom to think critically, the coloniality of my situation soon became apparent, and I began to understand what James Cone calls "a definite attitude . . . of an angry black man."[9] Truth be known, I was subliminally searching for a God who in the incarnation looked like me: Black. James Cone said so, it resonated with me, but I did not have permission to say so too. By which I mean I had not given myself permission to say so because the spoken and unspoken ecclesial understanding was that God in Jesus was not identifiable by ethnicity and color, which given the church to which I belonged had

---

6. Vincent, *Radical Jesus*, 97.

7. Vincent, *Radical Jesus*, 48.

8. Through his many writings John offered pointers to what this might involve, for which I found *Radical Jesus* most helpful, alongside two edited works—Rowland and Vincent, *Liberation Theology UK* and *Bible and Practice*—the latter in which, working with Garnet Parris, I contributed a chapter on "The Bible and the Black Church."

9. Cone, *Black Theology and Black Power*, 2.

almost (and in the case of the very top post of General Overseer) exclusively White people as head, meant subconsciously and consciously that if my colorless God in Jesus had to identify by a color, it was white, not black. In fact, any color except black.

As a lifelong Pentecostal Christian, focusing on the power of the Holy Spirit and salvation in the life hereafter, the question of my identity had been somehow obviated. Yet, to follow Jesus well, I yearned for affirmation of my identity as a Black human being made in the divine image and likeness of God. It was the introduction to liberation theology at UTU, with its focus on the dignity and humanity of the poor, that opened a door to this world of self-validation and self-empowerment. Although initially emerging from the Latin American context, bringing to the center people consigned to the margins by oppressive exclusionary practices resonated with my historic and contemporary experience of my people and me. UTU provided the space for me to agree with Cone's pronouncement that "God is Black" and the confidence to say and write so, because God is committed to and identifies with the oppressed.[10]

Neither Liberal nor Conservative: Radical

Up to this point, my epistemological lenses were mediated through my Pentecostal and denominational upbringing. Attempts to question, let alone deconstruct, inherited theological and ecclesial understandings were met with "These are headquarters' teachings, they cannot be questioned at individual, local, or even national church level, only at the General Assembly." Although such a tendency is unexceptional among Christian denominations, it nevertheless has the effect of shutting down questioning and stifling intellectual growth, since these are viewed as signs of disloyalty and disruptiveness emanating from a discordant spirit. UTU provided the tools to inquire into these and other matters.

Serious personal growth began with my introduction to the truly liberal and liberating space of UTU that did not require me to abandon my beliefs or my church, rather to freely interrogate them. Other Black Pentecostals studied at UTU, some predated me, some were fellow students, and some followed afterward, with varying degrees of success. I understand well why what John and others had created as an open learning and development space challenged us all and some fell by the wayside. Indeed, a few

10. Cone, *Black Theology of Liberation*.

who sought my advice about where to study and whether I thought UTU was suitable, I discouraged when I thought a confessional learning space might better suit. Those would-be students of theology who needed to be taught and instructed were not in my experience likely UTU students, and I knew the faith of some in their tradition, doctrine, and indeed in the Jesus to which they had been discipled would be unlikely to bear up under questioning—from their enlightened selves. As, Laurie Green, another UTU luminary, put it, like Jesus, growing up, maturing brings with it a new way of seeing.[11]

The UTU John created was for me a place for those who wanted to learn to swim and were willing to risk learning how to, theologically speaking. And yet, neither John nor any staff at UTU ever once questioned or ridiculed my traditional conservative Pentecostal faith. They merely helped me gain courage to wade out into the deep, as Jesus invited his disciples (Luke 5:4). The encouragement was to take risks to make progress across the sea of life, knowing one cannot swim or sail remaining with the certainty of the beach. Those of us from a Pentecostal background who encountered UTU fell into three main categories, in my view. By far the majority did not survive to completion. Then there were those who completed, received their certificates, closed the "books" (including their radical theses), went back to the comfort of conformity in their denomination, despite what they discovered. A third category, into which I—probably arrogantly—put myself, left UTU transformed and like Old Testament prophet Jeremiah could not keep quiet, because what they discovered was like fire burning unquenchably deep in their bones.

I realize now that my Christian ontological moorings never stopped being biblically and theologically conservative, to this day. I am what I am. I have not converted to biblical or theological liberalism. Instead, I have become questioning in an indiscriminatory way, questioning liberal theologizing and the inherent dangers of being the handmaiden for popular culture, and questioning conservative theologizing and the dangers of Luddite resistance to change. A consequence of this ecclesio-theological centrist disposition is that to conservatives I appear liberal, and to liberals I appear conservative. Probably the most telling impact of studying at UTU is the way it has orientated me toward a ministry of ecumenism based on mutual respect, tolerance, and commitment to allow others their theological and doctrinal beliefs as fellow followers of Jesus. In fact, my ministry

---

11. Green, *Power to the Powerless*, 8.

underwent a transformation from narrow tribal denominationalism to one of national Christian ecumenism—since studying with UTU, I worked for eighteen years for a combination of an intercultural education and ecumenical work, the Centre for Black and White Christian Partnership, based in the Selly Oak Colleges, Birmingham University; Churches Together in Britain and Ireland; broadcasting with the BBC and other outlets, such as the BBC's *The Daily Service*, *Pause for Thought*, and *Prayer for the Day*, as well as appearances on religious broadcasters like Premier Radio and United Christian Broadcast; writing, editing, and publishing. Included in all of the above is an emphasis on public Christian ministry in the mission of God in the world, not confined within a denomination or within the four walls of a church building. This wider gaze comes with inherent challenges as previously alluded to above, but with incalculable benefits. The relationships that ensue speak to building on the kingdom of heaven on earth, led by the example of Jesus. Respectful and enriched relationships by disciples of Jesus allow us to live as occupants of Jesus's mansion of many rooms (John 14).

A Base Community for Study

John and UTU have been nothing short of transformational for me as someone who had become stuck academically. Successfully writing and defending two 70,000-word theses had a profound effect on this deep rural bare-footed boy from Top Mountain, St. Catherine, Jamaica. I have attempted to write about my journey in a hurriedly compiled and under-researched autobiography.[12] I was able to achieve a dream of returning to the all-age school I attended prior to coming to England as "Dr. Joseph Aldred." And to share hope, resilience, hard work, a "never give up, never stay down, never lose hope" message with the children there at the time. Delayed but achieved academic prowess has not made me the brightest person on earth, but it has enhanced me in my context as a Black Christian person of African and Caribbean heritage living in England as a citizen with claim to dual citizenship.

UTU as a study base helped me discover my academic and theological self. I realized I could not recover years of inadequate academic information and formation, but I could use vast resources of lived experience to formulate views and thoughts and action about and in the present and

---

12. Aldred, *From Top Mountain*.

future. I realize that the theology I had encountered that effortlessly assumed universality was actually contextual European and American theologizing rooted in the indulgences of European Enlightenment, emerging from a comfortable existence of a supposed superior race lording it over their inferiors, especially the presumed bottom of the pyramid, Blacks.[13] I learned that I was sorely out of touch with African thought and had imbibed negativity about my own historical roots and the superiority of Western oppressive and imperialist, colonialist cultural norms that ignored or misrepresented the African roots of Christianity.[14] The emergent theology that I now relate to is one of all humanity rooted in the *imago Dei*, the agency and self-determination implicit in that, at work with the power of the example of Jesus in the wider community of humanity.

I remain eternally glad for the day that note popped through my letter box with its invite to visit John at the Urban Theology Unit. Like Jesus, John is a true revolutionary, changing not just things but persons, of which I am pleased to be a living testimony. Thanks, John! You invented White allyship long before the race industry's race warriors did.

Bishop Dr. Joe Aldred: Church of God of Prophecy, UTU graduate (MMin-Theol and PhD), ecumenist, broadcaster, writer, speaker

Bibliography

Aldred, Joe. *From Top Mountain: An Autobiography.* Hertfordshire, UK: Hansib, 2015.
———. *Respect: Understanding Caribbean British Christianity.* London: Epworth, 2005.
Aldred, Joe, and Garnet Parris. "The Bible and the Black Church." In *Bible and Practice*, edited by Christopher Rowland and John J. Vincent, 52–65. Sheffield: UTU, 2001.
Anderson, Allan. *Spreading Fires: The Missionary Nature of Early Pentecostalism.* Maryknoll, NY: Orbis, 2007.
Arnold, Selwyn E. *From Scepticism to Hope: One Black-Led Church's Response to Social Responsibility.* Bramcote, UK: Grove, 1992.
Boyd, Paul C. *The African Origin of Christianity.* 2 vols. London: Karia, 1999.
Cone, James H. *Black Theology and Black Power.* Maryknoll, NY: Orbis, 1997.
———. *A Black Theology of Liberation.* Maryknoll, NY: Orbis, 1986.

13. See Yeboah, *Ideology of Racism.*
14. See Boyd, *African Origin of Christianity*, vol. 1; Oden, *How Africa Shaped.*

Green, Laurie. *Power to the Powerless: Theology Brought to Life*. Hants, UK: Morgan & Scott, 1987.

Mbiti, John S. *African Religions and Philosophy*. London: Pearson Education, 1990.

Oden, Thomas C. *How Africa Shaped the Christian Mind: Rediscovering the African Seedbed of Western Christianity*. Early African Christianity. Downers Grove, IL: IVP Academic, 2007.

Rowland, Christopher, and John J. Vincent, eds. *Liberation Theology UK*. British Liberation Theology 1. Sheffield: UTU, 1995.

———. *Bible and Practice*. Sheffield: UTU, 2001.

Sealey-Skerritt, Dianne. *When God Calls: Listening, Hearing, and Responding*. Cambridgeshire, UK: Melrose, 2018.

Yeboah, Samuel Kennedy. *The Ideology of Racism*. London: Hansib, 1997.

17

The Testimony of Jesus: Anticipate the Ethics of the New Age

Chris Rowland

It was in the aftermath of a life-changing visit to Brazil in 1983 that I came back to England determined to find a way to emulate the relationship between my everyday job as a biblical theologian and everyday life such as I had witnessed going on in the basic communities in the shantytowns on the periphery of mammoth cities like São Paulo. John Vincent and the Urban Theology Unit had been mentioned to me, as had the work being done in Liverpool by Neville Black and colleagues in the Group for Urban Ministry and Leadership. Both have remained close friends. My first visit to Sheffield led to many more visits, several bringing groups of students from Cambridge, who themselves continued to have a relationship with UTU.

I shall not forget the first visit I made bringing the students, I think in 1985. During one of the sessions Ed Kessler contrasted the UTU core group with the Cambridge group, as the former being "disciples" and the latter being "saints." It struck me as a contemporary way of exemplifying what a New Testament interpreter like Gerd Theissen had written about the contrast between the lives of the first disciples of Jesus and the communities of the Pauline mission!

My times at UTU were always a learning experience for me, just as had been the time in Brazil, and they informed and enriched my work as a university teacher at first in Cambridge and then Oxford. In Brazil I saw biblical scholars working with and enabling people to understand life by means of the Bible, to quote a phrase of one of the people I met, and, just as important, learning from ordinary people the meaning of the biblical text. So it was not a matter of coming back and applying what I discovered, as if Brazil offered a blueprint for Sheffield. Rather it was a matter of listening and constructing ways of learning that arose from the challenges of those I met to unlock the wisdom and skills to enable understanding and action for justice.

Squaring the Circle

One of the problems of my intellectual life is that since the exposure to liberation theology I have been deeply attracted to it, but never quite able to keep up with the demands of a burgeoning academic discipline, which itself is viewed with a mixture of puzzlement and disdain by (supposedly) more hard-edged, traditional theological disciplines. It smacks too much of commitment rather than detachment, the intrusion of the interpreting subject into the scientific world of the academy.

I attempted to square the circle by finding places to engage in the kind of work with the Bible that I saw going on in Brazil and seeking to emulate the intellectual endeavors of the committed exegetes that I met in 1983, in Liverpool with Neville Black and his Group for Urban Ministry and Leadership project and in Sheffield with John Vincent at the Urban Theology Unit. What I discovered was that engagement with liberation theology does not translate into the research and writing that "counts" in the academy. Yes, I suppose I could have embarked on a Marxist interpretation of the Bible. I briefly tried that and was not convinced that it led anywhere, other than doing yet another desk-based study of the Bible to add to the more conventional ones. Anyway, the data required to do the historical task was not really available. That is why I found myself drawn to groups on the fringes of the mainstream Christian theological tradition, whose positions and priorities in many ways anticipated liberation theology. It seemed then, and continues to do so, that there is a rich tradition of grassroots reading of the Bible and social commitment, some of it completely unknown, which deserves a hearing in the groves of academe. So, squaring the circle of continuing New Testament interest and this diachronic historical perspective drew me to reception history and the way in which the Bible, especially the book of Revelation, has been treated through history and the radical biblical interpretations of William Blake and Gerrard Winstanley.

What I saw happening at UTU was born and bred in Yorkshire in two ways. First of all, there was the primary experience of having been born and brought up less than twenty miles away from Sheffield, in Balby, now a suburb of Doncaster, which in so many ways has colored my outlook on the world, not least that sense of unease about living and working in Oxbridge for forty years. I was delighted to learn that my part of Doncaster offered a space where the pioneers of the Quaker movement found a home just outside Doncaster, where there were those committed to nonconformist beliefs and practices![1] Second, UTU under John's aegis was the product of reflection on the experience of living and working in the inner city and allowing the Bible to inform that experience. UTU confirmed what I had learned in Brazil. That commitment is the challenge facing theology today, so that intellectual endeavor can be organically related to the issues facing us, whether that be climate change or the plight of people in a deeply divided society. That means not only that religion and politics must mix, but also being true to the biblical tradition. It means following in the footsteps of Amos, Isaiah, John the Baptist, Jesus, and countless others down the centuries who have understood life by means of the Bible, thereby enabling their contemporaries to see what made for their peace. Following that means working, like Paul the apostle, to create communities of hope amid a society all too easily tempted to ignore the fact that the well-being of all in society is crucial to its future.

Prophetic Commitment to Practicing Community

Prophetic witness and a commitment to a different kind of society with different values and priorities is at the heart of the New Testament and the heart of what a community of the new age is about. What all the New Testament writers have in common is the conviction that in Jesus, the new, messianic age, hope has come and is in the process of realization. But, as compared with the gospel stories, what we have in the Pauline letters is far more detail about what that means in practice. Jesus is represented as teaching his disciples, but the content of that teaching is allusive, in parables and related sayings and in predictions of his imminent death; but what led him to go up to Jerusalem and how the kingdom of God might come is left unclear. The disciples accompany him, following Jesus in the way (Mark 9:34; 10:32). Although passages like the Sermon on Mount (Matt 5–7; see

---

1. See Hoare, *Balby Beginnings*.

also Luke 6–7) contains much ethical teaching, not only are the narratives less prescriptive, but also there is less detailed instruction about the nature of community, with the possible exception of the practice of the forgiveness of sins, found particularly in the Gospel of Matthew (Matt 18:15–20; see also Mark 11:25), than the kinds of instructions and embryonic doctrinal system we find in Paul's letters. Paul, like Jesus and indeed John of Patmos, was dependent on an overwhelming apocalyptic experience.[2]

That led to a radical reorientation of his life. He became part of a minority community of solidarity and resistance to contemporary culture. In so doing he offered those who followed him a place that was on the brink of seeing something new. His letters give us a glimpse of a community organizer enabling individuals to learn to coalesce and manifest the characteristics of the new age which they hoped for. Of course, there are themes in these letters that are socially conservative and evince pragmatism, which helped lay the foundations of a pattern that was socially independent of mainstream Judaism even if parasitic on some of its tenets.

The contextual nature of Paul's theology has been widely acknowledged in Pauline scholarship, underlining the occasional and time-bound situated-ness of what is written. But even in the most conservative passages, where Paul sought to keep women subordinate or talked positively about the divinely ordained "powers that be," there is a recognition that, whatever change happened, it had to take full account of the constraints of context. While today we may chafe at aspects of the advice that Paul gives, the ways in which Paul seeks to find a space not only for himself but also his churches to live different kinds of lives amid a very different set of values is an amazing feat of survival and creative living. In effect, what he achieved was to set up an alternative political commitment characterized by practical and administrative arrangements manifested in networks of communication and mutual support. Paul's collection for the poor in Jerusalem is one of the earliest examples of this (Rom 15: 25; 2 Cor 8–9). It is a model for practical theology in any situation in its exploration and discernment of how best to exploit whatever spaces are available to offer a glimpse of what life in the kingdom of God might be like. As 1 Corinthians, epitomized in chapter 13, makes clear, Paul above all was keen to ensure that mutual respect was encouraged (Rom 15:25–9; 2 Cor 8–9). His activity, in person and in his letters, is an amazing feat of ingenuity, improvisation, survival,

---

2. Bennett and Rowland, *In a Glass Darkly*, 19–21, 38–49, 184; Rowland, *Radical Prophet*, 26–30; 37–44, 64, 85–86, 135–36, 145–46, 163–64, 169–70.

and creative living to find a space not only for himself but also his communities, to explore different ways of living that anticipated the age to come. So, Paul is the epitome of the practical, contextual theologian. Even the Letter to the Romans, the nearest Paul gets to it a systematic treatise, is shot through with the need to pave the way for a visit to people with whom he has had little contact. The recipients are treated to an extended apologia for his messianic convictions and how he bore witness to a vision of a different kind of public space. This letter lays out the requirement for those attracted by that messianic vision to explore how they actualized it here and now. It is all about how one lives in anticipation of a world where sorrow and sighing will flee away.

Disorientated Ecclesiologists

Revelation disorientates ecclesial readers of any generation. It stands alongside the Gospels of Matthew and Mark in problematizing the boundaries between insider and outsider, disciple and unbeliever. Nowhere can this be seen better than in the letters to the angels of the seven churches, most of which take an uncompromising line toward those who might think that they are on the inside. For example, it is the weak and those who are on the point of extinction, like the slaughtered lamb (Rev 5:6), to whom is held out hope. The faithful are not churches but prophets and witnesses who find themselves suffering "outside the gate" (Heb 13:12), where also their Lord was crucified (Rev 11:8).

There is one group of humans who seem to be commended—those who bear witness or prophesy. This turns out to be no easy task, just as such ministry was an agony for Jeremiah and other prophets (Luke 13:33). Revelation is insistent that the role of the martyr or witness is of central importance. Jesus of Nazareth is the faithful prophetic witness, and his followers have to continue that testimony of Jesus (19:10). In Rev 10–11, John is involved in the unfolding eschatological drama of the apocalypse, when he is instructed to eat the scroll and commanded to prophesy. Here, as in 1:19, there is a direct call to participate as a prophet rather than merely be a passive spectator. It is a commission that comes in a context of much urgency. Like the Lamb in Rev 5, who has suffered for his witness, the prophet takes the scroll and shares in the same kind of activity. In Rev 11 the prophetic role encompasses every aspect of life (and death). That was something experienced by all prophets of God (Luke 11:49), particularly Jeremiah, whose call is evoked in 10:11 (see also Jer 1:10). Prophets could expect a life of witness, suffering, and death, so that whether they lived or died, they would recapitulate what their Lord had suffered (11:8). In the story of Jesus the Holy City is the site of profanity, in which there is continued the rejection of the prophets (Matt 23:35–37). The Holy City is a place of profanity on the same level as Sodom and Gomorrah. It is no holy place. That can apply to churches and holy places anywhere. They are all potentially sites of human conflict and the possible profanation of God's way.

In the book John and Grace wrote, aptly entitled *Inner City Testament*, they say:

> Testament is an evocative word . . . a Testament . . . is a serious kind of book, one that records facts, places, dates, people, happenings, and occasionally dramatic, amusing or typical stories. . . . Testament is just what this person or couple or group have chosen to set down. They cannot deny it, it just happened some way like this—always it's warts and all, but also not missing the many splendoured thing. But not always explaining things, you'd have to say. It's a Testament to things that happened, not necessarily an Apologia justifying all of them.[3]

One thing that John and Grace might have added, which I am delighted to do, is that leaving a testament is also bearing witness, and giving testimony is the key to understanding what prophecy is all about. Following the example of the testimony of Jesus is exactly what I believe I encountered in John and Grace and in the work of all those linked with UTU.

The prophetic vocation of witness is for the church as a whole; though, in reality, the community itself is riddled with compromise with Babylon, as the letters to the angels of the churches indicate. The life of prophets is not one of niceness and respectability, therefore. The prophets are received as tormentors by those who cannot cope with God's justice and prefer not to acknowledge it (Luke 8:28). Revelation 13, for example, offers a terrible vision of the whole world seemingly following after in amazement (13:4) and worshiping the dragon. Prophecy is no hole-and-corner affair but attracts the attention of political power and its antagonism (so 10:11; see also Mark 13:9). The lack of concern for human dignity is evident in the refusal to bury the bodies of the prophets (Rev 11:8) and the profanity of the rejoicing over their deaths. The inhabitants of the world are under the

---

3. Vincent and Vincent, *Inner City*, 9.

misapprehension that the removal of God's witnesses will mean an end to torment. Beliefs of that kind are commonplace.

Texts like Matthew (especially Matt 7:21–23; 18:21–25; 25:31–46) and Revelation do not so much offer a precise description of what is to come but a means of gaining a different perspective on the world, which challenges neat assumptions about priorities, inclusiveness, and values in society. They are most disturbing for any ecclesiology. As the letters to the seven churches indicate, who is "in" and who is "out" is not at all clear. Those who are most confident (the Laodiceans [Rev 2:15–19]) turn out to be the least included. Confessing the name and being part of an ecclesial community is not what counts; what matters is whether one has worshiped the beast and drunk deep of the fornication of Babylon. Matthew and Revelation suggest that to be in Jesus Christ means to follow in his footsteps, engaging in acts of mercy to the outcast and, in humility, sharing the lot of those like the Son of Man, who had nowhere to lay his head (Matt 8:20). Confession and membership of a specific religious group is less important than nonconformity with the mores of the beasts and Babylon. Identification with the way of the Lamb who is slain offers an epistemological change, though it does not guarantee it. Neither text allows certainty or assurance of status or destiny. These texts do not allow readers to rest confident that they can be assured of ultimate vindication. There is an ambiguity in the refusal to allow that complacency in the face of judgment. The mix of parable, symbol, and narrative functions like metaphor should stop the attentive readers in their tracks by the disturbing juxtaposition and get them to think about the world from another perspective, another set of experiences.

Revelation is the least "churchy" text in the New Testament. Christ stands outside the door of the church, never to be co-opted to the values of those in the comfort of the ecclesiastical ghetto. The political and economic challenge Revelation presents includes the church members. They are not exempt from the judgment meted out on those taken in by the political and economic injustice of the imperial beast and its Babylonian culture. There is no escape from having one's nose rubbed in the brutality of imperial power and the harsh realities of the nature of the injustice of the political system of John's day, which is imagined and evoked in this awesome example of word-painting.

But that comes back to the sense of alarm that the book engenders. It is not that of a rather excited street preacher, who threatens people with hellfire if they don't turn to the Lord. It is more a warning to what passes for civilization, a warning that its structures are deeply flawed, and that the complacent can no longer see what makes for their peace. Seeming insensitivity serves a central purpose, aiming to waken people to what is happening. Business as usual is no longer any option. The coming of a new age does not come inexorably with better standards of living, often at the expense of the majority of the world's population or the depredation of its resources. The words of Jesus capture the sense of urgency and warning of the Apocalypse's imagery: "They were eating and drinking, and marrying and being given in marriage, until the day Noah entered the ark, and the flood came and destroyed all of them" (Luke 17:27). So what seems like insensitivity toward outsiders, and lack of respect for those who flee to the ark of the church, is but a warning that life cannot remain business as usual. As Walter Benjamin famously put it in the ninth of his "Theses on the Philosophy of History," the greatest apocalyptic text of the twentieth century (written at the beginning of the Second World War as he fled persecution by the Nazis):

> A storm is blowing from Paradise; it has got caught in [the angel's] wings with such violence that the angel can no longer close them. This storm irresistibly propels him into the future to which his back is turned, while the pile of debris before him grows skyward. This storm is what we call progress.[4]

The genius of Paul is that he engaged in an exploratory, experimental, exercise in advising and admonishing his communities. He wanted them to learn to live together, but also to explore what it might mean to be messianic or, as Paul would have it, to be "in Christ." This was an exercise in mapping out Christian practice rather than an embryonic attempt at systematic theology. What is striking about Paul's contribution, however, is how different it is from that of Jesus, at least as it is depicted in the extant sources. The gospel tradition says that Jesus might have taught his disciples, but the impression we are offered is of a group who were committed but increasingly either in the dark or puzzled about what was expected of them and indeed what would be Jesus's future. They followed him up to Jerusalem. "Let us die with him," says Thomas in the Gospel of John (11:16). It is so different with the Pauline letters. Not that there are detailed prescriptions, but there is evidence of a consistent attempt to assist in community formation and

---

4. Benjamin, *Illuminations*, 249.

guidance on how to live as a messianic age in the midst of an age passing away.

Paul was an apocalyptic rabbi, on the one hand a teacher who had a sense of authority and sought to impose what he thought on his communities, but on the other a man of vision, whose apocalyptic experience was the basis of his authority. Constrained by the limits of communication that confronted him as well as by his itinerant lifestyle, Paul inserted his written word into the midst of the nascent community in ways whose effects must have been electrifying. Words, theological ideas, and arguments tumble forth, all geared to try to enable groups of very disparate people to live together and to learn what an ethic in the face of the last days of this age might involve, to paraphrase the title of Don Cupitt's book *Ethics in the Last Days of Humanity*, in which Cupitt addressed the climate crisis as life lived in the shadow of an "impending crisis" (1 Cor 7:26). What Paul's letters bear witness to is that the messianic impulse is not just about the prophetic protest that points forward to a better world as it criticizes this one but also, alongside it, the patient, often painful, struggle to work out what it means in practice to embody that witness to the messianic age here and now. There is a necessary dialectic between community, indeed institution, however simple or complex that may be, with its necessary mutual responsibilities, always putting people first, and prophecy/advocacy. The latter role is the one that tends to be eclipsed by institutions, which can so readily be backward looking and self-serving instead of looking to a different better way of doing things with, and for, people.

Closer Than We Knew

If I have understood John right, he didn't need the catalyst of exposure to Brazil to revolutionize discipleship by reference to analysis of context and the way in which in New Testament times, as in our own practice, are formative of the understanding of the Bible, as the quest is made for a way of being disciples that is not only attentive to our situation but also gives centrality to the wisdom of all people, not least those who don't have a voice in society to the nature and priorities of discipleship. It makes me realize that I didn't need to journey four thousand miles to find context and experience being motors of engagement with the Bible and shedding light on it, as this was happening down the road from where I had been brought up.

Professor Chris Rowland: Emeritus Professor of the Exegesis of Holy Scripture at Oxford University, author, co-editor with John for the British Liberation Theology series

Bibliography

Benjamin, Walter. *Illuminations*. Edited by Hannah Arendt. Translated by Harry Zorn. London: Bodley Head, 2015.
Bennett, Zoë, and Christopher Rowland. *In a Glass Darkly: The Bible, Reflection and Everyday Life*. London: SCM, 2017.
Cupitt, Don. *Ethics in the Last Days of Humanity*. Salem, OR: Polebridge, 2016.
Hoare, Richard. *Balby Beginnings: The Launching of Quakerism*. Manchester: Sessions, 2002.
Rowland, Christopher. *Radical Prophet: The Mystics, Subversives and Visionaries Who Strove for Heaven on Earth*. London: Tauris, 2017.
Vincent, John J., and Grace Vincent. *Inner City Testament: Changing the World from the Bottom*. Sheffield: Ashram, 2017.

18

The Integrity of the UTU Method

Laurie Green

It is impossible for me to overemphasize the significance of John Vincent for my life and ministry. I had the good fortune to follow John to New York in 1968 and was alerted to his impact on New York Theological Seminary by my fellow students and particularly by its president, George "Bill" Webber, internationally famous for his creation and development of East Harlem Protestant Parish, about which books and a feature film were published. Bill had spoken of the seminary as being the hyphen between the Word and the world, and it was there that I saw experiments being undertaken in ministry and mission that during the intervening years have become common practice across the globe. Shop-front churches, issue-based churches, the emphasis on development of local leadership through rigorous and intellectually robust experiential training, the bringing together of Bible and existential issues like racism, classism, sexism, impoverishment, and so on, all ideas that today we would consider essential ingredients of any ministerial formation and training, and they were all coming to fruition at that seminary. Bill Webber and his team had moved across town from Union Theological Seminary to take over the then-ailing New York Seminary, because they saw there the opportunity to explore much more radical approaches than were allowed them in the very prestigious but establishment Union, and they therefore had brought with them the academic integrity of Union together with a yearning to build that into a more contextualizing approach—but more of this later.

First Impressions

During my year as a postgraduate student there, Bill and others impressed upon me that on my return to the UK it was important for me to meet John Vincent who, as I have said, had been at the seminary but had returned just as I had arrived. So on my return I made a beeline for John, who immediately welcomed me into his circle, despite my being so young and inexperienced. But John always had that way of encouraging youngsters who were just getting started, and what that allowed me to do was to sit in on some of the most exciting and remarkable meetings of that era, where John sought to sell to those who would listen his plan to set up a community of theological commitment, study, and action, and to place it alongside the poor in the inner city of Sheffield. He'd already earned his spurs as someone who was able to deliver on his radical proposals by making a name for himself in the peace movement and gathering those who were prepared to sacrifice their security for the sake of an opportunity to live out the implications of the radical gospel.

John, of course, had no need to prove his academic credentials either, because he had personally studied under the great Karl Barth (in German no less), had written papers that would cut the mustard in any academic establishment and more popular books aimed at stirring Christians to committed action informed by the radical gospel. I have no doubt that if John had wished to follow an academic career, he would soon have been awarded a professorial chair in the USA or in Britain. But this was not where his heart was—it had always been, and was to prove always to be, alongside the poor, fighting inequality and oppression. John was a man driven by a vision, and no one was going to stop him. It was exciting to be there with him and observe his strategies and his tactics, his failures and his astonishing successes.

I remember sitting in a Chinese restaurant in London surrounded by some of the great names of the day in the field of radical urban training such as Neville Black, Donald Reeves, Jim Punton, Tony Dyson, David Sheppard, and others, as John carefully spelled out his vision for what was to become the Urban Theology Unit, to be established in a house in Abbeyfield Road in Sheffield's Pitsmoor district. He was drawing on the Ashram Community he already had there to underpin the theological studies with committed community living and intended to draw together a residential community to enlarge that embedded community with students who would stay for maybe a year to undertake courses that he was designing and already offering. Roy Crowder was the "leader" of the ashram at that time, although he would have shied away from that title, for it was a small, intimate, and cooperative group living the simple life together and totally devoted to the needs of the marginalized around them in the locality. Roy brought an intellectual rigor, too, writing very accessible papers on dialogical education, introducing us all to the intricacies of the work of the educational philosophers; Ivan Illich's *Deschooling Society* and Paulo Freire's *The Pedagogy of the Oppressed* had only that year (1970) been published in English. Roy worked well alongside John, and between them, those of us who were around them were being introduced to some of the most recent and exciting thinking in the areas of education, culture, and theology.

Stirring Beginnings

The establishment of the UTU house in Abbeyfield Road was a winner but demanded of John and his new team a remarkable degree of hands-on practical skill and design insight. The cellars were transformed to include an office, print room, and the beginnings of a library of journals on every conceivable urban sociological and theological issue. Upstairs in the back room another library arrived, courtesy of the gracious gift from the widow of Alan Dale, the biblical scholar, translator, and writer. Both libraries continued to grow as more volumes were donated by others, and the rooms upstairs underwent ingenious conversion to accommodate the students, now arriving from all over the world, enticed by John himself, who was always on the road, encouraging, cajoling, and irritating Christians all over Britain and often further afield. It was his charismatic presence that won many adherents and converts to his radicalism. But John made it clear to all that his radicalism was not his own invention but came at us directly from the pages of the Bible and most particularly in our present context from the Gospel According to St. Mark—the gospel that he had studied in great depth through the years and where he found the most obvious and insightful correlations with the issues of our day. He was able to look with us at the text and see in it parallels, reprimands, and exhortations that not only set us thinking afresh about the text but struck us deeply in our guts as words that demanded our rapt attention and courageous response. And having had that experience for ourselves, John would ask each and every one of us, "OK, then what are you going to do about it?"

It was that stirring of the heart which was perhaps the most exciting aspect of our studies together in Sheffield, such that we were prepared to travel from all over Britain to attend the courses, even if we were not actually living in the community. For although the residential community was key to the work, there were many traveling in daily or for extended periods to be charged afresh by these experiences to continue their respective ministries and engagements back home within their own localities or areas of work. Others, like David Dale, were specialists in other disciplines altogether but fed into the work perspectives we would never ourselves have been able to provide. For me, the experience of UTU came at the very best moment, for I had already studied academic theology at King's London and had followed that up with a master's degree in New York and further studies back in Britain, but I was finding that those experiences had left me bemused and muddled as to how the learning from these conflicting styles of theology could possibly cohere. Additionally, I had been born and bred in the East End of London, within a largely Marxist family of committed union activists, and personally schooled by my Stalinist grandmother—so trying to come to terms with the Marxism I still harbored and its insightful analysis of oppressive forces in society and with the staid theology I had learned in Britain was tearing me apart. Academic theology was still being taught as a corpus of learning, a great fund of scholarship and the tradition of the ages, but had not Marx famously observed that "the Philosophers have hitherto interpreted the world—the task is to transform it"? Where then did any of those pious and metaphysical theological notions actually impact the poor and marginalized, or attack the oppressors and "bring down the mighty from their thrones" (Luke 1:52)? I had been steeped in Leninism as a youngster and especially warmed to Lenin's pamphlet *What Is to Be Done?*, and here at last was John Vincent offering me a way to work with all these, my earlier experiences, and seek some way to bring them together to make something coherent, meaningful, honest to Christ Jesus, and what's more, issue in respondent action!

John was presenting us all with a method that seems on the surface to be as simple as eating fish sticks. You look at the situation around you, you look at the stories in Mark's Gospel, and suddenly you're struck with an exciting similarity. Jesus heals a blind man, and we sit round in the group, seeing with newly opened eyes the realities of the power structures of our own locality. Jesus calls his disciples together, and likewise here we are working together to learn and follow his footsteps. Jesus lives a life embedded in the culture of the poor villages, and here we are seeking to minister in backstreet parishes all over Britain.

And so on it went. John likened the method to a children's game of Snap, where the playing cards are laid down by each player in turn until someone spots that one card is like the card that's just been played. John would ask us to do the same by playing with the issues raised in our locality with the issues raised in the pericopes of Mark's Gospel. And from that happy and humble beginning as a game of Snap, John had us all developing more sophisticated "ways in" to discovering what the dynamics of the gospel stories were and how they related to the dynamics at work in our lives, our work, our concerns.

A Suggestion, er, Expectation

I was keen to bring to bear upon that second side of the Snap game what I had learned from the models of social analysis at which the Marxist community activists were very adept, and also I had worked in mental health research and had picked up a lot of the tools of psychological analysis there. It was here that John Vincent once again set me on a track that would change my life. On seeing these interests, he suggested (well, John never exactly *suggested*; he *expected*) that I write up some of my approaches to situation analysis, and it was that prompting that led me to write my first "how-to" paper for other students. John was getting us all to offer our insights, and if anyone came up with something helpful or new, he would badger us until we were able to present it to a study group and thereby gain confidence to commit it to paper.

He would then get his backroom crew to type up the results onto a foolscap stencil (a large sheet of specially waxed paper) to be duplicated on the Gestetner duplicating machine. You could always tell someone had been working the UTU machine because their hands would be covered in the thick, slimy ink that would ooze out as the decrepit machine clunked its way through the print run. I always marveled at Margaret Mackley's ability to produce whole magazines, pictures and all, using the basic and testing technology of the day. But this was the way of it, and seeing our own contributions reproduced in type for other students to read gave each of us a great boost and the confidence to do even better next time—and all thanks to John's pushy initial encouragement.

There was nothing quite like a community of learning to urge us to develop new ideas, and the dialogical methodology used by the seminar groups was well informed by Roy Crowder's continued input and expertise. We'd assemble for a session, and John, usually late, would charge into the front room where we all sat around on chairs or the floor, drop down a pile of recent books and then charge out again, returning a little later to apologize that he'd just thought of something else he had to ask his already beleaguered office team to sort out. Then at last we'd get down to work. Very often it would begin with John wiping off the theological scribbles of the last session from the chalk board—only later replaced by whiteboard and pens—and begin to draw great diagrams to picture for us his latest thoughts or theories. Then we would all set to, rubbing out sections, adding in new insights, offering different perspectives, and affirming the central tenor of the resultant diagram. We'd then get to working with the model that we'd designed to see if it actually cashed out in practice, and we'd go away after a couple of days working on the results to ponder the emergent ideas in our own situations and see where they prompted liberative gospel action, returning a couple of months later to see where our model could be reworked and bettered accordingly. A few months later and John would publish yet another of his many books and there would be our model, together with all its possibilities, so that the whole world could benefit from each radical and exciting new adventure in active theology.

As the years progressed, certificates were awarded each new batch of students, new programs of learning developed to cater for different types of student, and there even came a time when different church denominations were sponsoring quite a large cohort of clergy trainees each year as part of their preparatory or ongoing education. John had, of course, not only to teach, attract assistant tutors, develop programs, and travel the country, but also to manage the complexities of administrative backup, housing maintenance, and much more besides. With Grace always at his side, it was a miracle to see how much the Vincents were able to achieve, with the establishment of local vegetarian and eco-shops, new shop-front or pub-front churches, and much more besides, making for a vibrant and visionary place to visit. We all came away inspired and determined to do more.

Does John Have Anything to Teach Us?

We must remember that, although we may look upon the established churches today somewhat pessimistically, they are streets ahead of where they were then. I was phoned, during those heady UTU days, by the archdeacon of the diocese in which I was working, because he was being encouraged to send more students to Sheffield, but in a very dismissive tone he asked me, "Vincent hasn't got anything to teach us, has he?," not realizing that he himself really hadn't got a clue about how a democratized theology can reinvigorate Christian endeavor. But that call presaged things to come as the major denominations began to redirect their funding toward more pedestrian and "church growth" programs. It was in time to prove a big financial hurdle for UTU, because without a steady churn of new students, it was going to be difficult to maintain such a large organization—but John was not daunted and ploughed on without a wrinkle in the radicalism of the programs. Besides the financial, there was, however, another side to the problem, because our central tutor team on UTU were concerned that if we had to shape our programs to suit those who paid the piper, then that radicalism, so fundamental to UTU, could well be compromised. We were all determined to back John and have none of that.

I was now aware that although I had been studying theology for most of my life, the shape and style of that theology had changed and developed considerably since those early introductions at London University. And now I needed to find a way to take stock of where I now was, to make sense of it, and to gain fresh direction for the years that lay ahead of me. It was personally fortuitous therefore that just at that time John came up with yet another of his mind-crunching schemes. Why not offer a program of study, utilizing the processes and radical models that we had developed, but now at a doctoral level, where the research backing the dissertation's thesis would be carried out not in an academic library but within the cut and thrust of parish life and the issues of marginalization and urban poverty?

He had ventured to go back to our alma mater to see if New York Theological Seminary could see a way of backing us with their professorial staff, their methodologies, and the locus of New York City. Being the radical outfit they were—and given the high regard in which they held John—they immediately responded by saying that, in principle, they were prepared to work with us and to have the doctoral degree awarded through New York University. Because we were to utilize such a radically new model, it could ride on the back of what in the States was called a professional doctorate, and the university would allow us to run a pilot group to see if it was a viable model for them and for us. John asked four of us from Britain and another from Kuala Lumpur to be in the pilot tranche, and with him and Dr. Dick Snyder from New York, we set to on our new theological adventure.

The work enabled me to look again at the Marxism of my youth, at British working-class history, especially at the work of Heidegger and the Frankfurt critical theorists, and then to engage the issues all that raised for my parish, taking as our springboard the parables of Jesus. Our parish group of local Christians and one Hindu, as it happened, worked its way through role-play, situation analysis, Bible study, and lots more, eventually producing an amazingly new approach to the theology of power and powerlessness—all worked through in practical outcome and much more theologically informed projects in the local community under Spaghetti Junction where we lived. I remember a leading light in the group remarking at the end of the program, "Before I met Laurie and this type of theology, I thought incarnation was something you got out of a tin!" Just that remark alone made all the hard work for the doctorate feel worthwhile, so as a tribute to them, I wrote it all up in a more accessible form to be published as *Power to the Powerless*, the *Church Times* review calling it the first real expression of liberation theology in a British context.[1] Not long after that, John set up the British Liberation Theology group so that we could all take that aspect of UTU's work further.

Two Legacies: Personal and Correlational (Snap!)

John's work with UTU continues, having already had an extraordinary influence upon the British church and vast numbers of Christians, but he also leaves a vivid legacy for tomorrow's church. He has been the pioneer of the democratization of theology, and additionally he has helped Christians to see the biting relevance of the biblical Jesus in ways that work in our hearts, our minds, and our actions.

But for me, two important aspects of John Vincent's many-faceted pioneering work contribute to his legacy. The first great contribution John has made to theology I might liken to the work of the person I take to have the finest theological mind of the twentieth century, Paul Tillich. Tillich had served as a chaplain in the trenches of the First World War and had been invalided out twice as his mind lost its equilibrium amid the horror of what

---

1. Edwards, Review.

was all around him. He had arrived at the front a strict, Prussian Lutheran, but all the certainties of the theology and beliefs he had come with had been shattered into a thousand pieces by the experience of the trenches. It had a similar effect upon him as it would have upon the thinking of Dietrich Bonhoeffer under similarly horrific pressures, of realizing that for most thinking people, the religious thinking that they had heretofore accepted simply no longer cut the mustard in this new bleak certainty of oppression. The God up there, at his safe distance from the world, but promising that all will be well in the by-and-by was clearly a myth that no longer had credibility. Tillich rubbished that, his previous conception of God, and in its place strove to understand how it could be that we experience the Holy, we have glimpses of divinity, not outside the world in some nether region but right here in the heart of our existence. Tillich could see that God was not "up there" or "out there" bemoaning our sinfulness but was right in the heart of our reality, suffering along with it and crying out from the mud-filled trench for justice and for peace. God is within our experience, not above it and untouched by it—the promise of the incarnation. And John, living in the downdraft of that wartime realization, knew that the world around him had changed irretrievably, and in the harshness of the inner city it was hard to sell all that old church stuff about a loving God "out there" who would give us a good time after death—with the proviso that we believe a set of doctrines devised by the church. John was determined to stay with the here and now to find God, not scamper off to the safety of "pie in the sky when you die," which was being offered by that old time religion.

    John knew God was Emmanuel, God with us, because he had personal heart-wrenching experience of it in the yearning faces of the suffering people he met in his pastoral work and in the shattering injustices he met in the dynamics of the society in which we live. He begged us to look at and analyze our situation not simply with the sociologist's interest but because he knew in his gut that we meet God there, right in the heart of it. Metaphysical supernaturalism as an answer did not convince the minds and certainly did not grab the heart of today's people, except as the illusion and escape that some ministers still offer when they begin their services with "Let us come away from this naughty world, forget your worries and concerns and meet God in this service." John has given us, as did Tillich and Bonhoeffer before him, the determination to look for the God within our experience.

    The second impactful legacy that John offers the future is that of "correlation" methods. That's the word Tillich uses for what energizes John's game of Snap—looking for the ways in which the Christian treasure store of myth and story and gospel event correlates with the issues and situations that surround us. They act, according to John, as "ways in" to the insights that we can use to overturn the powers and principalities. The realization that the gospel stories can shine such a penetrating light on our situations that we are graced with a new consciousness of the realities that the powerful try to hide is indeed a personal liberation, or "conscientization" as the jargon has it. The Jesus story enables us to see our present situations and problems so clearly that it not only focuses the mind more sharply but gives the Holy Spirit the space to get in and mobilize our energies so we can play our part in change—change of our perceptions and the perceptions of others—but also to effect change in the balance of the powers that hold people captive. It is, when I read Tillich, as if John Vincent has put flesh and bones around the journey of correlation that Tillich was eager for us to follow.

But as well as thanking John J. Vincent for the flowering of the wonderful legacy that he offers to Christians of tomorrow, I want finally to reiterate my personal gratitude to a man who has been for me not just a pain in the neck (if you know and love John as I do, you'll understand what I mean) but also a loving, caring, prompting, pressuring, creative, force of nature and ardent follower of the Jesus way. So, John, thanks for the memory but for much more than that—a bright, shining energy that has enabled us and generations to come to follow the gospel road to effective and penetrating liberation.

Right Rev. Laurie Green: DMin graduate, author of numerous books, former principal of the Aston Training Scheme, former Anglican bishop of Bradwell

Bibliography

Edwards, David L. Review of *Power to the Powerless*, by Laurie Green. *Church Times* (Oct. 16, 1987).

Freire, Paulo. *Pedagogy of the Oppressed*. Translated by Myra Bergman Ramos. New York: Herder and Herder, 1970.

Green, Laurie. *Power to the Powerless: Theology Brought to Life*. Basingstoke: Pickering, 1987.

Illich, Ivan. *Deschooling Society*. New York: Harper & Row, 1970.

Lenin, N. [Vladimir]. *What Is to Be Done? Burning Questions of Our Movement*. [In Russian.] Stuttgart: Dietz, 1902.

PART VII

Short Personal Tributes, Testaments, and Testimonials

19

Eye-Openers

Margaret Mackley

A "Come Down Our Way, Lord" weekend in 1978 introduced me to John Vincent, the Urban Theology Unit (UTU), Ashram Community, and the Sheffield Inner City Ecumenical Mission (SICEM). Like others of that era, I found that the Jesus I read about in the gospels was not the Jesus I heard about in the church, and I felt that I didn't fit in the church. Brought up as a Methodist, I had gone through Sunday school, youth clubs, and membership classes. I had become a local preacher and youth club leader, which was pretty much the pattern for a layperson who wanted to be involved with the church, unless you were one of the "powerful" group of people in the church who ran all the decision-making meetings.

The weekend in Sheffield in 1978 opened my eyes to so much, as John took us around SICEM. The five small inner-city congregations were small and vibrant and opened their premises to non-church people. The fact that they hadn't been closed because of small numbers remains with me today—just think sideways and find some allies to work with.

The two other members of SICEM were the Ashram Community House and the UTU, both of which John had founded—the Ashram Community in 1967 and UTU in 1969. Within both, I heard people using words such as justice, poverty, fair trade, inequality, campaigning, and the rich and poor divide. This wasn't just a lot of theorizing but practical action. I heard John talking about taking a journey downward, backward, and sideways, which I still throw into appropriate conversations, and talking about a radical Jesus.

So in 1979, when an advert appeared in the *Methodist Recorder* asking for people to come and live in an apartment above a corner shop in Grimesthorpe—to be the Grimesthorpe Methodist Church—I jumped at the opportunity. It was certainly a "journey downward," which I had to justify to many people. However, two days before I was due to go to Sheffield, I received a telegram from John saying, "Don't come yet as shop not ready." This was a most unusual thing for John to say, as he was always trying to get people to come to Sheffield! The next bit of the telegram said, "But come and do the Study Year instead, at UTU"—which was probably his intention all along!

I did what was known then as the Theology and Mission Integration course. It was challenging as you looked at your life history and analyzed what you did and why and reflected theologically on it. I found other people's stories fascinating, but I was so relieved to find that there were other people who thought like me and were frustrated by the traditional church in the UK. John's lectures were always stimulating, opening new ways of looking at the Jesus story, especially in Mark's Gospel. We were encouraged to visit the SICEM churches and be involved in their projects. Even today I have the situation analysis material at the back of my mind when it is suggested that a certain project might be a good idea.

In spring 1980, I moved into the Grimesthorpe apartment with Mark Woodhead and Richard Levitt, and in September 1979 started to do admin work at UTU and eventually became the coordinator overseeing the admin, houses, and finances for fourteen years. UTU was not at the forefront of modern technology, partly because of John's own lifestyle of living simply and partly because UTU didn't have much money. It was not easy working in the cellar, with old typewriters and Tipp-Ex, battery calculators and handwritten ledger books for the accounts, and looking out of a tiny window onto people's shoes as they walked up the path of 208 Abbeyfield Road. It was a luxury when we moved up to the ground floor of 208 and could see out onto the garden. I think by this time we had progressed to large computers and Excel spreadsheets!

I stayed at UTU until 1994, and through the people whom John invited to UTU I was able to get into things that I would never otherwise have had the opportunity to be part of—New Roots Shop, Vincent v. TSB, Pitsmoor Community Transport, local politics, SICEM employment scheme, Pitsmoor Youth Housing Trust, traveling to America to meet UTU members. But being at UTU enabled me to stay within a local church, use skills that

I gained while working with John, and look for like-minded people both inside and outside of the church.

Margaret Mackley: UTU graduate, ashram member, UTU administrator/ coordinator (1979–94)

20

Crossing the City

Frances Morgan

THE FIRST TIME I met John was around 1980. I was visiting him to find out more about the work of his churches and UTU for a school resource. Then we chatted for a while as I commented on some of the books in his library. I knew of UTU but had not been on a course, so he invited me to try one. I wasn't too sure it was for me; anyway, a while later I accepted the invitation. I can't remember details of this first course, but I do remember the relaxed and friendly atmosphere, the sharing of ideas, and it being relevant to a specific local situation. So I decided I would like to try out some other courses. Sometimes this was exploring familiar issues, at other times the subjects were new for me; sometimes there were familiar faces, at other times new participants. It always felt a friendly and safe yet challenging place to be, and there was plenty of time to chat over coffee and the shared meal.

Over two or three years I seem to have worked my way through most of the study year program, and John suggested if I did one more course, I would complete the diploma. That was when it became clear that where and in which situation you study can play a part in the outcome. It was the during the course on Mark's Gospel, which I had both studied and taught, that it became clear: just as "new cloth can't mend worn material," there are times when it is appropriate to live in a new situation. So, in 1984, I crossed the city and was able to be more involved with UTU; and the following year John invited me to join the core staff. I enjoyed this opportunity until 1993.

During this time I had many opportunities to contribute. One especially comes to mind. John had asked me to work with him on one of the new courses; I think it was called diploma in community and ministry. The participants had some meetings at UTU, but others were in their regional groups, and John and/or I would visit these gatherings, where we had the opportunity to see the areas where they worked.

In 1987 I bought two adjacent terrace houses about twenty minutes' walk from UTU. These would provide accommodation for three people in addition to me. A friend whom I'd met at UTU joined me, and gradually over time tenants were from various backgrounds, some having support from Community Services. Downstairs, one room was for several years an office for Ed Kessler, also a member of the core staff. Other rooms were available for local meetings and showed our involvement in the community. That was a valuable time for several years, but situations change, and by 1999 both houses were sold; and now the houses and street have gone.

From my first meeting with him, I realized John would often make a suggestion of a course or action, and I could choose how to respond. I found him a good listener, who supported me in my decisions. I think many people have found the same, as he has brought many people together over the years with different courses, sharing their varied experiences.

The Ashram Community was another example of bringing people together. I was able to enjoy weekend walks, summer holidays, and community gatherings: plenty of opportunities to share our stories, concerns, and joys, learning from others where their commitment had led them. I gradually realized I had entered a rich community of people from the city, the country, and the world. All this over the years led to new friends and experiences. I am grateful to have been able to play my part in it.

Frances Morgan: UTU graduate, ashram member, core staff (1985–93), chaplain to ministerial students

21

The Tale of Two Drew-Ids

John David Dillon

I WOULD LIKE TO offer my John story for this special project. John and I have theological degrees from Drew University in Madison, New Jersey; John has his STM from there (1956) and my MDiv is from there (1978), hence the "Drew-ids." In the fall of 1976 John was teaching at Drew, and I was smart enough to take what he had to offer. John's love of the Gospel of Mark opened so many doors into Mark, and that gospel came alive for me for the first time in my life. Not only is Mark "John's baby," but the way he explained it was infectious. But what really drew me to John was his special brand of kindness, a kindness that I had never encountered in anyone before that. Other encounters with John over the years and decades also were based in that kindness. It's in his smile still.

A true spiritual partner is one who encourages you to look deep within yourself for the beauty and love you've been seeking. A true teacher is someone who helps us to discover the teacher in ourselves . . . John has done this for me.

Rev. John David Dillon: UTU graduate

22

St. Francis House

Anne Scheibner

In 2006 Emmett Jarrett and Russ Carmichael were working together on the winter homeless shelter in New London, Connecticut. The three of us and my old friend and colleague, Geoff Curtiss, went to visit the Urban Theology Unit in Sheffield, England. Geoff and I had met through the Urban Hearings in Newark, New Jersey, in 1978 when I was on staff for the hearings and he was fresh out of seminary. Even then Geoff was connected with John and looking to develop a renewed vision of discipleship in the American context. John Vincent and his wife Grace were leading partners in the work of the Ashram Community based in Sheffield when we visited in 2006.

We had had a wonderful sabbatical time but really had not been in touch since then. That October, Grace Panko called me to say that Geoff had called St. Francis House. He and John would be in Manchester, Connecticut, the next day. Since they would be "in the neighborhood," could they stop by and stay with us on Monday night? They ended up staying with us until Wednesday, and what a joy it was to reconnect!

John and Geoff attended our Tuesday study group. John launched into telling his story of being a graduate student under Karl Barth in Basel. There he had had to make a decision to go with a discipleship-driven understanding of church. Barth had disagreed with his position but encouraged him to stand fast in his faith. Each of us seated at the table was challenged in turn to share our "snap" moment of understanding our own personal calls to discipleship. It was a riveting exercise. I am still thinking about the implications for the work of St. Francis House and how tempting it is for me even in this setting to get lost in the "dreary desert sands of dead habit," as Rabindranath Tagore wrote.[1]

So, what is the shape of discipleship communities today? On the morning of their departure, John left me a handwritten reflection, which we decided to adapt for a lead article for the *Troubadour*, the newsletter of St. Francis House. We at St. Francis House continue to explore what "church" is for us at this point in history.

Anne Scheibner: Lived and worked at St. Francis House, New London, Connecticut

Bibliography

Tagore, Rabindranath. "Gitanjali 35." Poetry Soup, 2020. Translated by Michael R. Burch. https://www.poetrysoup.com/poem/rabindranath_tagore_gitanjali_11_1220885.

---

1. Tagore, "Gitanjali 35," line 6.

23

Embodying the Radical Spirit

Richard Firth

I FIRST HEARD ABOUT John by repute. I was training at Wesley College, Headingley, Leeds (1961–65), alongside a fellow student from Rochdale who spoke glowingly of John's radical approach to ministry at Champness Hall in the town center. This preceded his move to Sheffield since when all is history! My next acquaintance with John was through his books. As a young minister starting out, I read *Christ and Methodism: Towards a New Christianity for a New Age*. This and his many other subsequent volumes greatly influenced my own approach to ministry.

In 1989, when John was president of the Methodist Conference, I was superintendent of the Gateshead and Jarrow Circuit and privileged to host one of John's day conferences entitled "Nearing the Nineties," designed to focus on relevant issues: how to be Methodists now, finding Jesus in today's society, new forms of church life, mission alongside the poor, theology and politics; all subjects perennially pertinent. The event closed with a service of celebration in the largest church in the circuit packed to the rafters.

In retirement I decided to become a student at UTU, wanting to keep the grey cells active! I researched Methodist worship, a subject that I had never studied before even though having led it for more than forty years! John, partnered by Eric Wright, became my main tutor. Under his guidance I experienced the most stimulating nine years of study. Seminars were never run of the mill but always challenging, compelling ever to think outside the box.

Long may the radical spirit, as embodied in John's life and work, flourish within Methodism and beyond.

Rev. Dr. Richard Firth: Methodist minister, PhD graduate, UTU trustee

Bibliography

Vincent, John J. *Christ and Methodism: Towards a New Christianity for a New Age.* London: Epworth, 1965.

24

Completing the Circle

Andrea Misler

Meeting John for the first time in 2009 at the Othona Community, Essex, I was really in awe. Somebody who had actually known Karl Barth, even better: Barth had been John's *Doktorvater* along with Oscar Cullmann. As a German, the name Karl Barth was theology at premium league: *the* systematic theologian of the last century. I could not have been more impressed. And then he invited us for the Eucharist in words so simple, so welcoming, and most of all so inclusive that everyone attended, in a community that is open to all faiths and none.

John made many things seem simple. He invited me to write my PhD with him at the UTU. I had no idea at that time what he was talking about (qualitative research, auto-ethnography, Lebenswelt, participant observer, observant participant, etc.). So when I came to Sheffield under John's aegis I had to relearn. He first sent me to volunteer in the Burngreave Ashram shop in what I would call a precarious area. Cooking with people with mental health difficulties was on the agenda. I thought to myself that I could run the shop so much more efficiently, not understanding at that time that the shop was not about efficiency but about a low-threshold meeting place where openness and acceptance prevailed. John taught me to put into words what my community and I had been doing for decades. He and Ian K. Duffield in particular encouraged me to tread the road less traveled in order get to the bottom of things. I had to consider issues that I had never in my life given a thought to: my Germanness or indigenous theology, for example.

With the help of John's practice interpretation (a new approach to the gospels on what first listeners/disciples make of the gospels in their lives) I remember a moment of glory when my students realized that the "stilling of the storm" (Mark 4:35—5:1) actually had something to do with them. They could well relate to and identify with the boat, the disciples, the storm, and the other side. Our discussions would have no end.

I have always felt that I was closing the circle: John starting off his career with his PhD in Basel and two German-speaking *Doktorväter* to him, finishing it by being my *Doktorvater* (me as the only German ever at the UTU with a PhD and two English-speaking *Doktorväter*). Or is it rather balancing the equation? John and Ian have both shown me that learning is exciting at any age.

Thanks for that. John, *vielfachen Dank. Der Weg zum PhD war ein Fest. Gottes Segen.* Andrea

Dr. Andrea Misler: Member of ashram and the Othona Community, PhD graduate

25

The Best Colleague

Ian Lucraft

JOHN VINCENT CAME TO Durham Methodist Society in June 1968, and I was a student then in the congregation. I was studying sociology and politics and candidating for the ministry of the Methodist Church. I knew nothing of him, nor can I remember what he preached about. What I do vividly remember was that John had clearly not realized we were at the point in the service where the offertory was expected, and as he was bending down behind the pulpit to reach for a book, without rising to his full stature, he looked up over the pulpit from a bending position and said, very directly but casually, "We'll collect the offering." I immediately warmed to his lack of piety or pomposity. I had not seen such in my teens in the church. I still have the book *Here I Stand*, given to me that day, I think, according to the inscription, by the student chaplain, Rev. Martin Eggelstone. I now realize of course that John almost certainly was carrying a box of them for sale after the service. It formed the basis of one of my earliest sermons while candidating. I reread the sermon recently and would be happy to use it again, over fifty years later!

My next encounter with John was only five years later. I had gone through Handsworth and Queen's, and was on probation in Chapeltown, in Leeds, at the wonderful Roscoe Place Methodist Church, under the mentorship of Rev. Trevor Bates, to whom I owe a lot. I was really nervous about what opportunities might be available, as it was clear that after a two-year probationary appointment I would have to move on to vacate the place for another student. But where? I dreaded a rural or suburban circuit and did not know how to ensure a city place. Someone showed me an advert that John had put in the *Methodist Recorder* for an appointment in Pitsmoor, in the new Sheffield Inner City Ecumenical Mission. I later found out that he was well out of order doing this, as he was crossing the stationing system, and I think he got his knuckles rapped for it. I applied and, after interview, was thrilled to get the post. More surprising still was that I later heard I had been the only candidate for the post. How could there not be a queue of young ministers for such an exciting and interesting and challenging post? Someone shockingly explained to me that not many people would want to work with John.

Of course the situation was surrounded by turmoil. Before he came to Sheffield he had done a guest speaker service, Home Mission or something, in the beautiful Burngreave Road Methodist Church. It had recently been rebuilt, unbeknownst to him, after a bomb had destroyed the church in 1942. He was there to talk about his ideas for the church of the future. He stood up and said, "They should have dropped a bomb on this place!" Even now I can't imagine the shock and outrage of the congregation. And then to find a year or two later that he had been appointed, against his will and theirs, to be the minister in that station. But within a couple of years, he had helped the two local congregations to see that their future would exist in the area only if they merged and rebuilt. And the woman who had raised the money for the war-damage rebuilding, Amy Richinson, one of the church leaders, was the first to say, "I think John is right." Not only was the church turned upside down, but a new circuit was carved out in the inner city to be a safer place for the small inner-city churches that the more suburban churches wanted to close. Turmoil indeed.

But here I was, invited to join a small team and be appointed to a new united congregation in a new building. I have often thought that not many ministers would have fought for a new congregation and a new building and then hand them over to a young man just ordained. Which only goes to show how wrong people could often be about John. Yes, he could be iconoclastic, but always rooted in the gospel, the call to make the church fit for the age, and to focus disciple activity on justice and faithfulness. Yes, he could be abrupt, but he never meant to be rude; he did not have time for mealymouthed circumlocutions. Yes, people sometimes wondered how the funds managed to stretch to maintain the fragile existence of the mission; but John was always scrupulous about the source and application of funds. Creative, yes. Imaginative, yes. Leveraging resources wherever he could, yes. But always accurately accounted and used for the purposes given. I never knew an honest man so badly maligned by people who did not like him, or did not "get" him, or misunderstood his theology, which was more closely aligned to the words and actions of his Lord than many of his critics understood about him or themselves. What they also didn't get was that under the surface, he is a sensitive and gentle man, compassionate, and sometimes insecure himself, though not often visibly. And no one close ever underestimated how important Grace was to his ability to be the person he was throughout his working life, nor did they miss the immense but discreet pride, he had in each of his children and the love he had for them all.

As a colleague, he trusted me to get on with what I was appointed to do. We had some moving and challenging staff meetings but never dreary. We laughed and wept together on occasions. We backed each other up to the hilt and brooked no denigration by others. We were evangelical about the place of small churches in the impoverished communities in which they were struggling to survive. We were angry at the institutional church when it tried to apply business rationales to the location and support of marginal churches.

I was immensely privileged to be alongside UTU and Ashram, though carefully not "of," them as my role was different. I shared in so much of their thinking and even more of their rich cultural mixing of people and ideas from around the world. People came from all over to sit at his feet. Sometimes the great man showed that he had feet of clay. His single-mindedness could put people off or cross their own pathways, and they would walk away, sometimes in anger. More often, people saw and shared his insights and understood how they would drive forward their own path of faith and ministry. Sometimes they would quietly go their own way afterward but still use that insight and depth of faith to empower their own ministry. Some stayed for many years. John stayed true to his commitment to the place he had been appointed, and now fifty-five years later, he is still there, having given his all to the place and the people he loved.

Others will speak of his writings and his teaching and his political campaigning. I want to say that he was the best colleague I ever had. I loved our bouncing ideas off each other. I loved being creative in ministry and mission, and he was always way ahead of me. It became what we would now call a "meme." We would be at a meeting and agree that something would happen. It would be faithfully recorded in the minutes. And from that moment on, it was if it had already happened. There was a real gospel urgency about making the future of the church and its disciple groups. The phrase "prophetic foreshortening" emerged. If a new creation was written down, then it has already happened. There were certainly prophetic echoes.

Each of us had priorities and blind spots. I was always trying to reconcile my understanding of the realities of physics and science in general, and creationism in particular, such that I was moving away from any sense of a God who acted for good or for creation. I had no difficulty in Jesus the man, but it was the God thing that always got in my way. For John, I was never sure where he was in actual fact in that discussion, but I do know that he was absolutely certain that it was not a conversation that profitably took us anywhere. Look at the stories and words of Jesus, and live them in your own life—that was his determination.

Most of all I remember sitting in my little Citroen car after we had driven home from some meeting. We were lost in the depths of a conversation about faith and belief and understanding and were unaware of the time, parked there on Abbeyfield Road. One of those moments of utmost clarity and openness and trust. We were talking about how we are called to "be" the Christ for others, perhaps not as ministers but certainly as Christians. Even though we had failings and doubts and all the rest. I remember looking at him and saying to him, as I realized that this truth was even deeper in him, "You think you are Christ for others, don't you?" "Yes," he said. It was an electric moment. And then something like "But don't repeat that, as people will misunderstand it." I've reflected on that one sentence all the rest of my life, and I think he was right. Of course he was right to be cautious, as many incorrectly thought him arrogant, and this would only play into that prejudice about him. He was never unaware of how people saw him. But he was right. "Being" Christ is not a simulacrum, a way of acting. It is the definition of ourselves as Christ for others. Jesus the man invites us each to "be" Christ for those in front of us. The sense of the Christ being a spiritual expression of the holy Jesus is not enough. It has to be real; it has to be us, with all our imperfections.

John, I will love you forever, for all that you have been for me. Sometimes I had to distance myself from you to maintain my own sense of self. Sometimes I had to disagree with you. Sometimes I had to walk away from you and leave you in the lurch, which I will always regret. But you have inspired me throughout my ministry. I have always been proud to have worked alongside you. You helped me to see that obsession can be very productive. And throughout, I knew we were OK with each other. Thank you.

Rev. Ian Lucraft: Methodist minister, John's colleague in Pitsmoor

Bibliography

Vincent, John J. *Here I Stand: The Faith of a Radical.* London: Epworth, 1967.

Biography

John James Vincent

John James Vincent was born on December 29, 1929, to David and Ethel Vincent in Sunderland. His mother described the day as "wintry" and that "the doctor and nurse had to walk quite a distance, but I had a dear friend with me. She was a splendid and a great comfort. We had another dear little son!"[1]

That entry hints at the kind of person John would eventually become: resilient, adaptable, and ultimately cheerful.

He came from working-class people—and entrepreneurial. His father, David, grew "tired" of being a shop manager and started a new business in Altrincham. While John learned to carve hams on Saturdays, he also learned the art of fellowship and congregational life, particularly its singing and music. From his mother, he learned piano, artistic expression, and an appreciation for the arts, with many trips to the ballet, theater, and opera during the later war years. "Mother and I seemed to be 'on the same wavelength,'" according to John. "We instinctively understood one another." John was born into a world exhausted by war: "Britain was sparse in every way . . . but the sparseness said that you must create meaning and value within yourself. This meant for me art and reading."[2]

At eighteen, and just before joining the army, John was invited to an SCM Congress in Westminster:

> Two memories of speakers remain: One is the brilliance of Reinhold Niebuhr. But, even more I recall the passion for the poor of Father St. John B Groser. More significant was that, together with another student, I took off for two nights which we spent in the

---

1. Vincent and Vincent, *Inner City Testament*, 12–13.
2. Vincent and Vincent, *Inner City Testament*, 14.

Old Kent Road, talking to street sleepers and people running soup kitchens. I knew that I had to become an inner-city minister. But I told no one.[3]

Read that last sentence and you might hear an echo of Mark 16:8, the shorter ending of the book that would captivate John's thinking for his lifetime. It recalls the experience of the two Marys, who after finding the empty tomb and the young messenger, react with such wonderment or fear that, at least initially, they choose to keep the secret they are no longer mandated to keep: "And they said nothing to anyone." Of course, the not-so-subtle irony of Mark's Gospel, and John's appropriation of it, is that someone eventually let the "secret" out—and maybe the empty tomb supplies a clue to what might be and what could be possible if we would give the kingdom of God a go in our community.

More of that in a moment. In 1958, John married Grace Johnston Stafford, daughter of the late Rev. Wilfred Stafford. Grace was born near Hyderabad, India, where her father, Rev. Wilfred Stafford was stationed as a Methodist missionary. Grace moved to Northern Ireland sometime around 1945. Grace and John met while out on a Methodist "day out" in the Peak District. Together, they had three children: Christopher Vincent (1961), born in Manchester; Faith (1964), born in Oldham; and two years later, in 1966, James, their youngest, was born, also in Oldham. Christopher credits Grace, his mother, with "providing Dad with endless day-to-day support and bringing us up." As she held the family together, and simultaneously contributed to John's ministry and theological writing in the inner city, she also taught English as a second language in a range of schools.

In 1960, John completed his doctoral thesis, "Discipleship in Mark," at Basel University, Switzerland, with Karl Barth serving as one of his supervisors. As a thesis it marked John's lifelong fascination with Mark's account of a radical Christianity embedded with the poor and the struggle for opportunity and equity. As you will see from the appendices, John maintained a prodigious publishing agenda. However, unlike some, John's writing not only reached academic circles but also grew from communities engaged with a variety of discipleship projects. His work was variously described as "correlation between text and context born in action"[4] and a British-shaped

---

3. Vincent and Vincent, *Inner City Testament*, 15.

4. EverybodyWiki, "John J. Vincent," s.vv. "Scholarship on Mark and Discipleship," citing Lawrence, *Word in Place*, 22.

movement analogous to the "earliest years of liberation theology in South America."[5]

This collection largely reflects the legacy of John's role as mentor, friend, community organizer, and scholar—and that is as it should be. But connecting something of his youth and love of communal singing and poetry offers an additional window into John's thinking. The introduction to the *Hymns of the City* (1989) offers a glimpse of the revolutionary spirit that John carried forward in every mode of his communicating, whether academic or congregational or street-based:

> The revolutionary good news of Jesus Christ is that a new reality—God's realm or God's kingdom, [Jesus] called it—is present in the midst of human history and that precisely that reality demands and deserves a total change in human practice, creating revolutionary new alliances, and releasing into world history a force of egalitarianism, commonness and mutual love which shatters all existing systems and creates islands of liberation.[6]

John understood his work as bearing on the transformation of society. But in a more personal, almost evangelical way, he carried on with the spirit of an underground (and singing) revolutionary. He declares:

> Disciples of that same Jesus exist today. They want to release this earth-changing activity and dynamic into the world. Some of these disciples who see this radical new promise live and work at the bottom of our society. They especially know this good news. And they need others to hear it, at every level of society.[7]

You may hear in that excerpt a key that resonates with the clarion call of evangelical conviction minus the straitjacketed soteriology that often conditions it. John's message was that God loves the world and seeks to release it from its captivities through the proclamation of the kingdom of God.

When he explains the origin of this collection of hymns, including pieces by himself, Fred Pratt Green, John Bell, and Margaret Mackley, among others, he relates a conversation he had with an editor of a recently published hymnal: "There are no hymns from the inner city or the poor," he said.

---

5. EverybodyWiki, "John J. Vincent," s.vv. "Scholarship on Mark and Discipleship," citing Shannahan, *Voices from the Borderland*, 101–7.

6. Vincent, *Hymns of the City*, 3.

7. Vincent, *Hymns of the City*, 3.

The editor replied, "There are none, are there?"

"Not yet," replied John. Never satisfied to point to an absence, John then committed to the work of a hymnal (several, in fact—see bibliography in the appendices) that grew out of those contexts. This is how he introduces the commitments of *Hymns of the City* (1989): hymns are from and for inner-city and estate churches; hymns are about real experiences of people and not the "endless 'Praise' for no particular reason, as seems to be the custom of the affluent churches"; hymns are mainly about Jesus Christ, especially his "starkness" and "angularity" and "unexpectedness" and ministry alongside the poor, put in a style that is "suited to urban survivors and prophets"—there is "little room for abstract concept or general humanist goodwill"; and in a nod to his down-to-earth approach to "making a new song" the words are put to well-known tunes. "Hymns," he declares, "are political statements as well as marching songs."[8]

Fred Pratt Green's "anti-carol" opens the collection with words set to the tune "Cradled in the manger meanly." It begins with an unsparing assessment of the status quo until, at last, the final stanza calls for the repair of our human economic and political relationships so that when we sing our alleluias and glorias, we do so in challenge to despair.[9]

While John's editorial influence is felt on the traditional tunes, his own creative turn was evident in his adaptation of the Red Flag anthem of the Labour Party, which it adopted at its founding.[10] The first stanza of the Red Flag anthem offers a glimpse into the way John happily tweaked the boundary between secular and sacred, infusing the "sacred secular" tunes with a kingdom of God message and, similarly, revising sacred hymns that were so heavenly they were no earthly good.[11]

There was always something "experimental" in John's practice of discipleship—and James, their youngest son, currently living in Brooklyn, NY, offers this insight into that dimension of life with their father:

> John lived his mission not just through writing books or making speeches, but by living his values by moving us to depressed inner city Pitsmoor in Sheffield, just as its industry was collapsing and

---

8. Vincent, *Hymns of the City*, 3–4.

9. See Fred Pratt Green, "All They Wanted Was a Shelter," in Vincent, *Hymns of the City*, 5.

10. "Red Flag" is set to the tune of "Tannenbaum," a German folk tune unrelated to Christmas but rather a comment on the evergreen fir tree's constancy. Later it became associated with "O Christmas Tree."

11. See "God's Kingdom's Flag Is Deepest Red," in Vincent, *Hymns of the City*, 9.

then sending us to local schools in the middle of council estates. His writings can be seen in the context of the new "radical" thinking sweeping every facet of life in 70's Britain. It was a fresh approach to institutional Christianity and an attempt to create more relevant and contemporary dialogues. John possessed a powerful control of oratory and the written word that helped to galvanize the communities that formed around him. He always used whatever fame he accumulated to serve the cause in a remarkably selfless way. Growing up with John and with our equally remarkable mother, Grace, in the Vincent household in the '70s felt like being a part of a radical social experiment. It honestly created some unexpected dilemmas for us as kids, but also gave us the strong determination to battle through adversity through the rest of our lives.[12]

Until very recently, John was still supporting the teaching of UTU's Certificate of Mission, Theology and Discipleship. Today, John has stepped away from active teaching, but his spirit of experimentation, radical discipleship, and willingness to give the kingdom of God a go lives on—and this is testament that many of us heard of that many-splendored thing in Sheffield.

Rev. Dr. Robert P. Hoch-Yidokodiltona, director of Theological Studies, UTU (July 2021 to present)

Bibliography

EverybodyWiki. "John J. Vincent (Theologian)." Everybody Wiki, last edited Aug. 1, 2020. https://en.everybodywiki.com/John_J._Vincent_(theologian).

Lawrence, Louise. *The Word in Place*. London: SPCK, 2009.

Shannahan, Chris. *Voices from the Borderland: Re-Imagining Cross-Cultural Urban Theology in the 21st Century*. Cross Cultural Theologies. London: Equinox, 2010.

Vincent, John J., ed. *Hymns of the City*. Sheffield: UTU, 1989.

Vincent, John J., and Grace Vincent. *Inner City Testament: Changing the World from the Bottom*. Sheffield: Ashram, 2017.

---

12. Email from James Vincent to Christopher Vincent, Sept. 15, 2024; permission from James to share.

Select Bibliography[1]

John James Vincent

Authored

Christ in a Nuclear World. Manchester: Crux, 1962.
Christian Nuclear Perspective. London: Epworth, 1964.
Christ and Methodism: Towards a New Christianity for a New Age. London: Epworth, 1965.
Here I Stand: The Faith of a Radical. London: Epworth, 1967.
Secular Christ: A Contemporary Interpretation of Jesus. London: Lutterworth, 1968.
The Working Christ. London: Epworth, 1968.
The Race Race. London: SCM, 1970.
The Jesus Thing: An Experiment in Discipleship. London: Epworth, 1973.
Alternative Church. Belfast: Christian Journals, 1976.
Disciple and Lord: The Historical and Theological Significance of Discipleship in the Synoptic Gospels. Sheffield: Academy, 1976.
Doing Theology in the City. Sheffield: UTU, 1977.
Strategies for Mission. Sheffield: UTU, 1977.
"Doing Theology." In *Agenda for Prophets: Towards a Political Theology for Britain*, edited by Rex Ambler and David Haslam, 123–34. London: Bowerdean, 1980.
Alternative Journeys: Gospel Calls for the Eighties. Sheffield: UTU, 1981.
Backyard Seminary. Sheffield: UTU, 1981.
Starting All Over Again: Hints of Jesus in the City. Geneva: World Council of Churches, 1981.
Into the City. London: Epworth, 1982.
"Towards an Urban Theology." *New Blackfriars* 64 (1983), 4–17.
O.K., Let's Be Methodists. London: Epworth, 1984.
"O.K., Let's Be Methodists." In *Radical Christian Writings: A Reader*, edited by Andrew Bradstock and Christopher Rowland, 280–84. Oxford: Blackwell, 1984.
Britain in the 90's. Peterborough, UK: Methodist, 1989.
Discipleship in the 90's. Peterborough, UK: Methodist, 1991.
"A Community Called Ashram." Sheffield: Ashram Community Trust, 1992.
Hope from the City. London: Epworth, 2000.

1. Arranged in chronological order.

Select Bibliography

The Covenant Service. Buxton, UK: Church in the Market Place, 2000.
Journey Resource Book: Explorations into Discipleship. Sheffield: Ashram, 2001.
"New Faith in the City." In *Faithfulness in the City*, edited by John J. Vincent, 290–306. New York: Monad, 2003.
Radical Jesus: The Heart of Radical Discipleship. Sheffield: Ashram, 2004.
Outworkings: Gospel Practice and Interpretation. Sheffield: UTU, 2005.
"Outworkings: The Practice of Disciples." *Expository Times* 116 (2005), 155–59. https://doi.org/10.1177/0014524605051865.
Discipleship—the Heart of Discipleship in Mark's Gospel and How We Can Get into It Today. Sheffield: Ashram, 2007.
A Lifestyle of Sharing. Sheffield: Ashram, 2009.
"Outworkings: Urban Mission in Mark 4." *Expository Times* 122 (2011), 531–38. https://doi.org/10.1177/0014524611409633.
Christ in the City: The Dynamics of Christ in Urban Theological Practice. Sheffield: UTU, 2013.
Radical Jesus: The Way of Jesus Then and Now. N.p.: Little Red Tree, 2014.
Jesus the Radical: Saving the World. Sheffield: Ashram, 2019.

Co-Authored

Davies, John D., and John J. Vincent. *Mark at Work.* London: Bible Reading Fellowship, 1986.
Vincent, John J., et al. *Gospel in the 90's: A Theological Disputation.* Peterborough, UK: Methodist, 1990.
Duffield, Ian K., et al. *Crucibles: Creating Theology at UTU.* New City Special 14. Sheffield: UTU, 2000.
Kimbrough, S. T., et al. *Urban Mission: Two Viewpoints.* New York: Global Ministries, United Methodist Church, 2001.
Hooker, Morna D., and John J. Vincent. *The Drama of Mark.* Peterborough, UK: Epworth, 2010.
Rogerson, J. W., and John J. Vincent. *The City in Biblical Perspective.* Biblical Challenges in the Contemporary World. London: Routledge, 2014.
Vincent, John J., and Grace Vincent. *Inner City Testament: Changing the World from the Bottom.* Sheffield: Ashram, 2017.

Edited and Co-Edited

Stirrings: Essays Christian and Radical. City Soundings. London: Epworth, 1976.
A Community Called Ashram. Sheffield: Ashram Community Trust, 1992.
Rowland, Christopher, and John J. Vincent, eds. *Liberation Theology UK.* British Liberation Theology 1. Sheffield: UTU, 1995.
———. *Gospel from the City.* British Liberation Theology 2. Sheffield: UTU, 1997.
———. *Liberation Spirituality.* British Liberation Theology 3. Sheffield: UTU, 1999.
———. *Bible and Practice.* British Liberation Theology 4. Sheffield: UTU, 2001.
Faithfulness in the City. New York: Monad, 2003.

"Basics of Radical Methodism: Challenges for Today." In *Methodist and Radical: Rejuvenating a Tradition*, edited by Joerg Rieger and John Vincent, 31–49. Sherborne, UK: Kingswood, 2003.

Rieger, Joerg, and John Vincent, eds. *Methodist and Radical: Rejuvenating a Tradition*. Nashville: Kingswood, 2003.

Mark: Gospel of Action; Personal and Community Responses. London: SPCK, 2006.

Christian Communities. Sheffield: Ashram, 2011.

Stilling the Storm: Contemporary Responses to Mark 4:35–5:1. Blandford Forum, UK: Deo, 2011.

Acts in Practice. Practice Interpretation 2. Blandford Forum, UK: Deo, 2012.

Rowland, Chris, and John J. Vincent, eds. *For Church and Nation*. British Liberation Theology 5. Sheffield: UTU, 2013.

The Farewell Discourses in Practice. Practice Interpretation 4. Blandford Forum, UK: Deo, 2015.

Rowland, Chris, and John Vincent, eds. *Radical Christianity: Roots and Fruits*. British Liberation Theology 6. Sheffield: UTU, 2016.

Methodism Abounding: Theology and Mission for the Twenty-First Century. Buxton, UK: Church in the Market Place, 2016.

Rogerson, John W., and John Vincent, eds. *The Servant of God in Practice*. Practice Interpretation 6. Blandford Forum, UK: Deo, 2017.

Hymnbooks

Parker, Robin, and John J. Vincent, eds. *Community Worship*. Sheffield: Ashram Community Trust, 1977.

Vincent, John J., ed. *Community Worship Revised*. Sheffield: Ashram Community Trust, 1987.

———. *Hymns of the City*. Sheffield: UTU, 1989.

Vincent, John, ed. *Community Worship 2000*. Sheffield: Ashram Community Trust, 1999.

www.ingramcontent.com/pod-product-compliance
Lightning Source LLC
Chambersburg PA
CBHW060606230426
43670CB00011B/1997